The
Embroiderer's
Garden

The Embroiderer's Garden

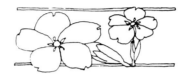

Thomasina Beck

with line decorations by Sarah Siddall

The garden is a work of art, not of nature
Humphry Repton

A DAVID & CHARLES CRAFT BOOK

To Christopher Thacker,
L'Amateur des Jardins

CONTENTS

INTRODUCTION

The pleasures of gardens and embroidery are so remarkably similar that it is no surprise to find that the garden enthusiast and the embroidery enthusiast are often one and the same person. Few activities offer such equal delight to mind and eye, and stimulate and absorb us so freely and for so long. If we are happy they receive our happiness and give it back again, if the world seems against us they are uniquely comforting and soothing; and we may enjoy our embroidery, or our gardening, in solitary state or with companionable friends, as we choose. Vita Sackville-West considered love, taste and knowledge essential for successful garden making, and I think the same applies to embroidery. For the plants, earth, water and stone of the real garden, embroiderers substitute their own richly varied materials from the thickest wools to the finest silks – they are indeed 'gardening with silk and gold thread' as William Morris put it. But whatever form their embroidery takes they need to cultivate an eye for line and form, colour and texture, as keenly as any maker of gardens.

The real garden is so fascinating to plan and to make because it is different from the world beyond. You can see this in any painting or photograph of a garden which includes a view of the surrounding countryside. It will be most obvious with formal gardens, whose regular patterns stand out from the natural landscape, but it is equally true of informal or even wild gardens where, despite their apparent naturalness, water, plants and groups of trees have been most carefully sited. Whether your garden is large or small, formal or informal, within it you, the gardener, are in control; you impose your patterns on the ground. 'Patterns' brings us back to embroidery, but just as the real garden appeals because it is different from the outside world so the embroidered garden appeals because it is different from the real one. Here you are in a world of your own, unrestricted by problems of labour, expense and space. In your embroidery you can create the longest vistas, the most fantastic topiary, the grandest parterres, and you can try out not one, but any number of knots. If your actual garden has

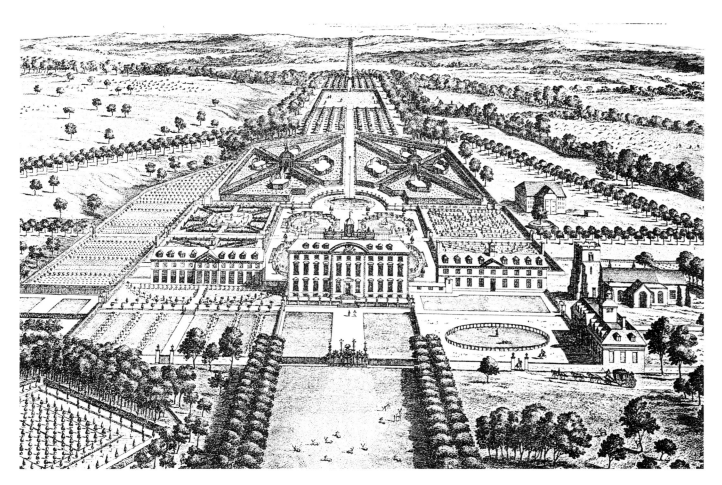

6

'Munstead Wood and the Hut as they may have appeared in 1901.' In Richard Sorrell's watercolour, the garden made by the much loved and influential Gertrude Jekyll stands out in contrast to the surrounding woodland. The main border in the foreground illustrates her skilful use of colour, graduating the shades from cool blues to bright flame in the centre. Nearer the house she tries out harmonies of violet and blue in beds of Michaelmas daisies. Embroidery inspired by her garden can be seen on page 15.

left Knyff and Kip's view of Wimpole House in Cambridgeshire (*c1707*) shows the contrast between the garden patterns and the natural countryside.

Christopher Lloyd, well known for his inspiring garden books and for the imaginative planting at his home Great Dixter in East Sussex, is seen here in the garden with his mother, Daisy Lloyd, displaying the canvaswork windowseat they embroidered together for the Great Hall of the house. They began one at each end and met in the middle where an argument ensued as to who should complete the last leaf. 'Who won?' I asked him. 'She did, of course', he replied affectionately. Embroidery inspired by the garden can be seen on page 31.

Seventeenth-century tulips including striped varieties from Besler's *Hortus Eystettensis* of 1613, one of the most decorative flower books ever printed.

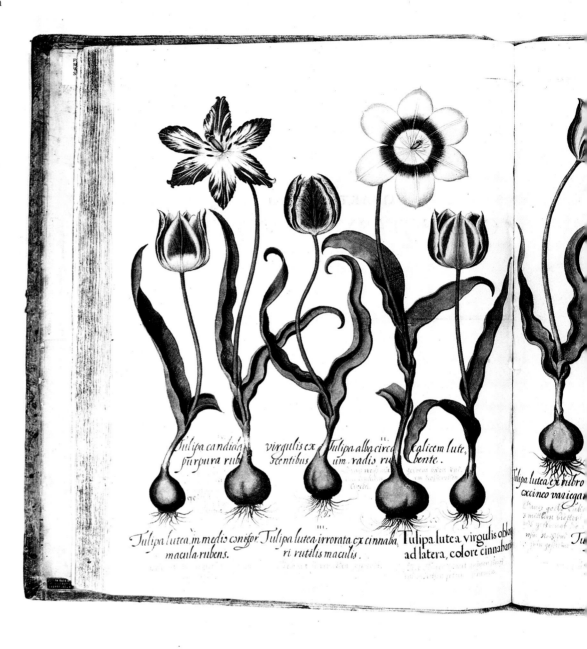

become too large and too demanding to enjoy, in your embroidery you can take refuge in the miniature world of the sink garden or alpine house you would so much prefer. And if your garden is too small to accommodate the old-fashioned roses that seduce you each summer, you can try to translate the radiance of those reds and the intensity of the pinks in stitchery, balancing the tones harmoniously so that if, one day, you do have the space outside, your garden colour scheme will be that much more subtle and assured. Similarly if you are, as I am, intrigued by the shapes and curious markings of the old striped and fringed tulips whose rarity makes them costly and hard to find, you can in needlework bring together and arrange varieties to rival any seventeenth-century collection.

If the garden is one of the richest sources of inspiration for embroiderers, so, conversely, embroidery can add a further dimension to garden enjoyment. It is a way of extending garden pleasure – your's and other peoples' – and it also offers a welcome change of tempo from the activity of the outdoor garden. Here you can experiment at leisure, unperturbed by the seasons and the weather. Unlike the lawn which has to be mown or it will become a hayfield, or the fruit that must be picked or it will rot on the tree, embroidery can be taken up when it suits you best and done at your own pace. It can evoke your own or other peoples' gardens, or it can be entirely imaginary and a way into the garden of your dreams – a tiny golden key like the one which enabled Alice to open the little door into the garden bright with flowers which she had glimpsed from the dark hall when she fell down the rabbit hole and which she longed to enter. 'And then – she found herself at last in the beautiful garden, among the bright flower-beds and cool

Tulip design by Joan Drew from *Embroidery and Design* (1929).

Red and damask roses from *La Clef des Champs* by Jacques le Moyne de Morgues (1586).

Rose design from *The Craftsman's Plant Book* by Ralph Hatton (1909).

fountains': Lewis Carroll's description might indeed be the inspiration for an embroidery of brilliant summer flowers framed in a dark doorway, or you might chance on a real garden scene so strongly reminiscent of it, and of your own childhood memories, that it sparks your imagination and makes you long to translate your experience into embroidery.

Gardens are among the most transitory, yet most enjoyable, of human creations, and the desire to perpetuate them is strong. Their transience is a deeply felt part of their appeal, like our own childhood, or the childhood of our children which is gone 'almost before we knew it was there'. Through our embroidery, we can, in our modest way, make time stand still.

Enthusiasm is the first essential, but that does not necessarily solve the problem of getting your ideas into workable form. The problem for embroiderers, especially for those who have little experience in making their own designs, is how to get started, and the aim of this book is to encourage their enthusiasm and show how the simplest attempts can lead to lasting and pleasurable results. Whether you are a complete beginner or have been doing embroidery for as long as you can remember, the willingness to learn and experiment is essential and part of the fun. As Gertrude Jekyll put it: 'The grand way to learn, in gardening as in all things else is to wish to learn and to be determined to find out – not to think that any one person can wave a wand and give the power and the knowledge.'

'The Carter's Garden in Greenwich' by Eugenie Alexander. Collage depicting the maker, her husband the artist Bernard Carter, her son and Tiggy the cat looking out of the house at their colourful garden. Beads and surface stitchery add interest to the applied shapes of wisteria, roses and clematis.

'Portrait of Sir Roy Strong' by Polly Hope. Machine embroidery, quilting and appliqué are combined to record the sitter's enthusiasm for his country house and garden. Over his shoulder can be seen the armillary sundial in the Jubilee Garden with beyond it statues of Cosmas and Damian and an eighteenth-century urn backed by yews.

Design from the title page of *Wood and Garden* by Gertrude Jekyll. The small illustration on page 6 is from her *Wall and Water Gardens*.

1

GETTING STARTED

Our England is a garden, and such gardens are not made
By singing:- "Oh, how beautiful", and sitting in the shade.

C. R. L. Fletcher and Rudyard Kipling,
A History of England (1911)

However keen you are to get started, it is sensible and enjoyable to begin by building up a stock of illustrations and information to help you choose suitable subjects, select materials and work out designs. In *The Education of a Gardener* Russell Page, one of the few great garden designers of our time, gives advice that is especially apt for embroiderers: 'Garden designers, like all artists, need nourishment; they need to exchange ideas, to study plans and photographs of new work and to visit gardens; in short, to acquire an education and a wide documentation.'

I first read this inspiring, original and at the same time highly practical book twenty years ago when I had just moved into a Tudor priory at the bottom of a narrow valley. The house and its setting were romantic to a degree – it had originally belonged to the Abbess of Shaftesbury and a secret passage led out of the cellars into a field up the valley – but the garden did nothing to add to this quality, and I felt at a loss as to how it could be reshaped to match the beauty of the house and its setting. Searching for help in Russell Page's book, I was cheered to read that, if choosing a site, he would prefer a 'hollow to a hilltop'. On the strength of this I wrote and asked him to advise me. He agreed, and the day I spent in his company was one of the most rewarding and instructive of my life. As we moved round taking measurements one at each end of a long tape, I saw the idea of the garden being deftly reshaped by the rapid jottings of his pencil as he explained, with a series of sketches, how I

should anchor the house to its setting and narrow the view to make it more mysterious. My budget was small, but this was understood from the start, and the garden was transformed by altering the proportions of the existing terrace, borders and paths to create the deliberate and coherent plan which every garden, however informal, must have. In embroidery it is just as essential to get the design right at the outset, and to spend time and trouble working out pleasing proportions, as no amount of fine stitchery will disguise a clumsy or ill-balanced plan.

To get your eye in to good design, garden books old and new are a prime source of nourishment, and it really does pay to immerse yourself in them. The writers quoted in this book have a particular appeal to the embroiderer because they often see and describe the garden and its plants in textile and needlework terms. Gertrude Jekyll, Vita Sackville-West, Russell Page and Christopher Lloyd frequently do this and they combine their advice with personal reflections, anecdotes and comments which make you feel they are talking directly to you and are eager to share their experience and persuade you to try out their suggestions. At a creative level, books make you appreciate just what a complex, challenging, but endlessly rewarding and fascinating business garden making is, and for practical purposes the wide range of illustrations in them are a marvellous source of inspiration and designs for all types of embroidery.

The formalised flowers and small pool with enclosing pergola in this bird's eye view from *Gardens: Their Form and*

Design suggest a treatment in contemporary stumpwork with flowers in needle lace and box edging in plush stitch.

The bold style of Mary Campion's illustration resembles appliqué and speckling stitches. This view of a paved garden is one of many striking pictures from *Gardens: Their Form and Design* written by Frances Garnet, Viscountess Wolseley, in 1919.

The linear quality of the drawing in this view of a modernist garden at Hyères in France by Gabriel Guevrekian immediately suggests machine embroidery or blackwork.

opposite 'The Grey Garden' by Elizabeth Ashurst. Machine embroidery on hand-dyed semi-transparent fabrics based on Miss Jekyll's photograph above of her Grey Garden at Munstead Wood 'so called because most of its plants have grey foliage, and all the carpeting and bordering plants are grey and whitish. The flowers are white, lilac, purple and pink'. To get the feel of Miss Jekyll's planting and colour schemes the maker visited restored Hestercombe near Taunton where she made notes and drawings for the embroidery.

Miss Jekyll's photograph of her Grey Garden at Munstead Wood with two of her plans for the borders of lilac, white, pink and purple flowers. The feathery artemisia in the foreground sets off the more distinctive shapes of holly-hocks and echinops, both seen in the embroidery opposite.

On this page of the Bodleian manuscript of 1504 the leaves of the small alder and aspen trees seem made for appliqué work. The exposed roots could be treated decoratively in quilting or couching and the daisy motif, like all the flowers, butterflies and birds in the manuscript, makes charming patterns suitable for many different methods.

I remember my excitement when I first came across a book called *Flowers and Trees of Tudor England* by Clare Putnam (1972) which was full of naïve but decorative drawings of plants – small stumpy trees and formalised flowers – reproduced from the pages of a manuscript dated 1504 in the Bodleian Library in Oxford. Having had no formal training in drawing or design, I was finding it extremely difficult to put on paper, let alone on material, the designs I wanted to embroider, but here was a whole variety of simple motifs which could be traced and arranged in any number of ways suggestive of gardens. At the time I was studying the flowers on Elizabethan cushions, which closely resemble the beds in gardens of that period, and I decided to make a set of 'garden' cushions based on the designs in the book. I wanted to recreate the slightly raised effect of the Elizabethan flowers which were worked in tent stitch on linen and then cut out and applied to a satin or velvet ground. As I was learning machine embroidery at the time I transferred the motifs to dupion mounted in a hoop, and filled in the flower and leaf shapes using the zigzag on my sewing machine. They were then applied to a heavy cotton ground. As the set progressed I found this simple quick method remarkably versatile in rendering leaf veining and petal markings in bands of closely worked satin stitch. If you have not tried machine embroidery, do experiment to see if you like the effects of texture and line – quite unlike hand embroidery and often well suited to garden subjects – which it produces. Practically everyone finds it difficult to start with, but do persevere. Like learning to bicycle it is a knack which, once mastered, is not only speedy but immensely satisfying and fun to do.

I began with a single motif and then worked out simple repeating patterns. I found similar motifs in the herbals and early flower books, but these are such a wonderful source of designs for garden embroidery that they must have a chapter to themselves. Their use is mentioned here as a way of getting over the stumbling block of feeling that you cannot draw well enough to devise pleasing individual designs.

I agree with Roger Fry, one of the twentieth century's most original designers, who said that 'in the long run it is not nearly so important whether an artist himself invents a motif as what he makes of the motif once it has come into existence'. It does not matter if you have only a limited range of stitches to begin with, but it is important to be able to work them easily and well. A single stitch is often just as effective as several – if not more so – and you could work the Tudor flower and tree motifs in couching, or an outline stitch such as stem or split stitch.

Embroiderers, like gardeners, enjoy sharing their experience, not only in books, but in lectures and classes as well. If you want to widen your range of stitches and learn an old-established or a new technique, join a class or day school where you can follow a method through and see the varied solutions other people find to problems similar to your own. Supposing, for example, you are struck by the violet-blue harmonies of delphiniums standing out in the summer border. The flower spikes rise in columns of bright colour, and their solidity contrasts with the lighter, less distinct flowers and foliage round them. A background of subtle varied greens would bring out this contrast, but where would you find such a fabric? Now might be the moment to experiment in dyeing and spraying your own background material – calico is a good inexpensive choice – to give you the necessary variations in tone (see page 56). But what type of paint or dye should you use, and how should you apply it?

Cushion designs based on the trees in the Bodleian manuscript opposite.

'Delphiniums at Chelsea Flower Show' by Janet Galloway. Here variety of tone and texture is achieved by dyeing the different fabrics and combining heavy machine stitching with straight hand stitches in cotton, silk and linen threads. The petals are silk cut out and applied and the leaves are cotton on a furnishing material ground.

'Delphiniums Blue' by Julia Barton. Panel inspired by the line 'Delphiniums (blue) and Geraniums (red)' in A. A. Milne's poem 'The Dormouse and the Doctor'. It is carried out entirely in chain stitch which gives unity to the design. Note how the direction of the stitches emphasizes the upright growth and how the use of metal and wool threads, repeated in the wrapped borders, creates textural richness on the subtly painted silk ground.

A photograph from *The Earth is my Canvas* by Percy Cane (1956), describing his career as a garden designer, provides the basis for an embroidery design using tracing paper to simplify the outlines.

The range of products has never been more exciting for garden embroidery, but it can be confusing too, as it is when you are confronted with too great a choice at a garden centre, and you remain uncertain whether your purchases are really appropriate to your garden's needs. In a class you can see the paints and dyes demonstrated and try them out to see which suit your purpose best.

But you may be the kind of person who prefers to work out solutions quietly on your own, sometimes making errors and finding that these lead to new possibilities. If, for example, you decide to try out some transfer paints or crayons which are used on paper first and then transferred to a synthetic ground by ironing, you may inadvertently overheat your iron and end up with areas of creases and puckers which add considerably to the textural interest of your ground! On canvas you could work the delphinium spikes in lustrous silk and the foliage in matt threads, which would act as a foil to the bright flowers. It makes sense to try out the stitches and threads first on a small piece of ground, then, if they do not seem appropriate, try looking at some of the methods used by embroiderers in the past to render a similar subject. In the Stoke Edith garden hanging, look at the foliage of trees and shrubs worked entirely in tent stitch most inventively patterned to evoke the variety in natural growth. When you look at historical embroidery in museums, houses open to the public, antique shops or sale rooms (do not neglect the sale rooms, not necessarily to buy but to see) and your eye is taken by a particular piece, try to assess why the chosen method works so well and note it down in case you want to experiment with it yourself on a different scale or with different colours. The same applies to contemporary embroidery where old methods are being constantly revitalised and new materials – dissolvable fabrics (see page 55), plastic mesh, transfer paints and dyes – open up new possibilities.

Look closely at photographs, drawings and paintings too. Black and white photographs in books and magazines can provide a useful basis for design as your eye is not distracted by colour, and can concentrate on tone and shape. Here again tracing paper is the embroiderer's best friend; if you place a sheet over your photograph, you will see how it blurs unnecessary details and defines shapes and tones of trees, plants, areas of grass and water even more clearly, enabling you to follow their outlines with a felt-tip pen and create the beginnings of a working design. A photocopy machine can be helpful too, not only in enlarging images to exactly the size you need for your design, but in emphasizing the tones still further, sometimes to the extent of making them resemble actual stitches.

Taking photographs of your own garden is especially instructive, as the camera lens automatically puts an outer frame round the various possibilities before you, and helps you decide what to include and what to leave out – often one of the most difficult aspects of making a design. It is amusing to watch a group of keen photographers in a great garden working out the most telling viewpoints and then impatiently waiting for the others to move out of the way so that they can record them; some photographers, however, will search out their own personal garden pictures which, for embroidery purposes, may vary in scale from an overall view to a close-up study of blades of grass encroaching into paving.

You can train your eye to be more selective through the camera lens, and you can take this selective process a stage further by enlarging your pictures and moving two L-shaped pieces of card (an old mount or matt cut in two) over them to frame exactly the area you want, which you can then trace and transfer to your ground.

Certain artists have a particular relevance to the embroiderer in their treatment of the patterns, textures and colours of the garden. The Swiss artist Paul Klee, for example, was passionately interested in plants and gardens and his impressions of them often resemble patchwork, blackwork or fine machine embroidery with neat rows of spiky flowers and tiny angular trees. Stanley Spencer emphasized the patterning and texture of grass, topiary, foliage and flowers in his native Cookham, lovingly recording them in minutest detail.

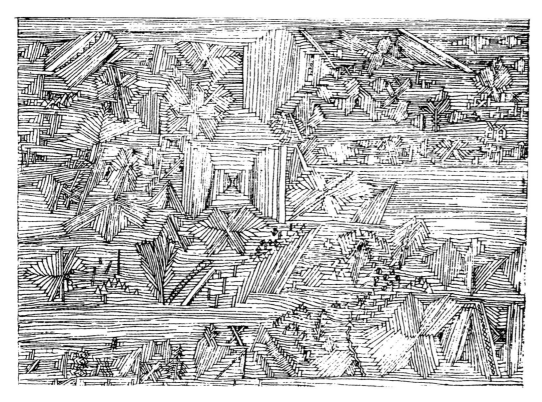

In this detail of 'Orpheus Garden' by Paul Klee (1926), the resemblance to blackwork and the patterns of log cabin. patchwork is striking (© COSMOPRESS, Geneva, DACS, London 1988).

'The Stoke Edith Orangery', one of a pair of large-scale early eighteenth-century hangings recently conserved and now in the care of the National Trust at Montacute House in Somerset. The garden laid out in front of the fashionable orangery includes many of the features discussed in this book. It shows how effective and sophisticated tent stitch can be for shading and patterning the surface of grass, sand, water, stone, brick, topiary and trees.

The two couples enjoying the garden, and the macaw and pet dogs in the foreground, bring the scene alive and stir our interest both in those who made and those who embroidered the garden. Their presence evokes the mood of that garden on that particular summer day, striking an appealing personal note comparable to our response to the contented domestic scene in 'Summer Sunday' captured on page 171.

Many of the impressionists painted their own and their friends' gardens, painting out of doors while they experimented with rendering the endlessly-changing effects of light and shade on flowers and foliage. The great colourist Monet was an obsessive gardener, constantly acquiring new plants and working out new colour schemes. Visiting his garden at Giverny, sympathetically restored in the last few years, it is easy to be overwhelmed by the profusion of bright colours. You can try to keep them in your mind's eye, but you would do better to note those that strike you as particularly telling or daring, like the rivers of nasturtiums in every imaginable shade of orange that edge the broad central path under the dark yew walk, and which are even more remarkable seen from the upper floor of the house, framed in the mauve painted window with its frilled muslin curtains piped in red. He saw them too – and captured them, their colours, their exuberance within the framing archways along the path. A part of the joy of visiting his garden now is to compare *his* paintings, with the present garden scene which *you* might wish to capture through embroidery.

'A note book is a most important companion on gardening expeditions', wrote Mrs Earle in her delightful garden diary *Pot-Pourri from a Surrey Garden* (1897). 'On first going into a garden one knows by instinct, as a hound scents a fox, if it is going to be interesting or not. One's eyes are sharp, and a joyful glow of satisfaction comes over one on seeing something not by any means necessarily new, but unknown to oneself.' She was especially keen on recording what she called 'intelligent gardens' and recommended making small coloured sketches of plants; these she found a great help to the memory, having come to gardening so late in life that, as she said, 'I had to get all the help I could'. The more you visit gardens the wider your knowledge and your understanding will become, especially if you try to develop a searching eye for elements that in some way suggest embroidery. However much you are seduced by individual plants, always try to consider the design of the garden. If you do this when visiting great gardens you really will, albeit

The delightful motifs in the Bodleian manuscript can be used singly or combined to make simple designs. They can easily be worked in outline stitches and are ideal for beginners.

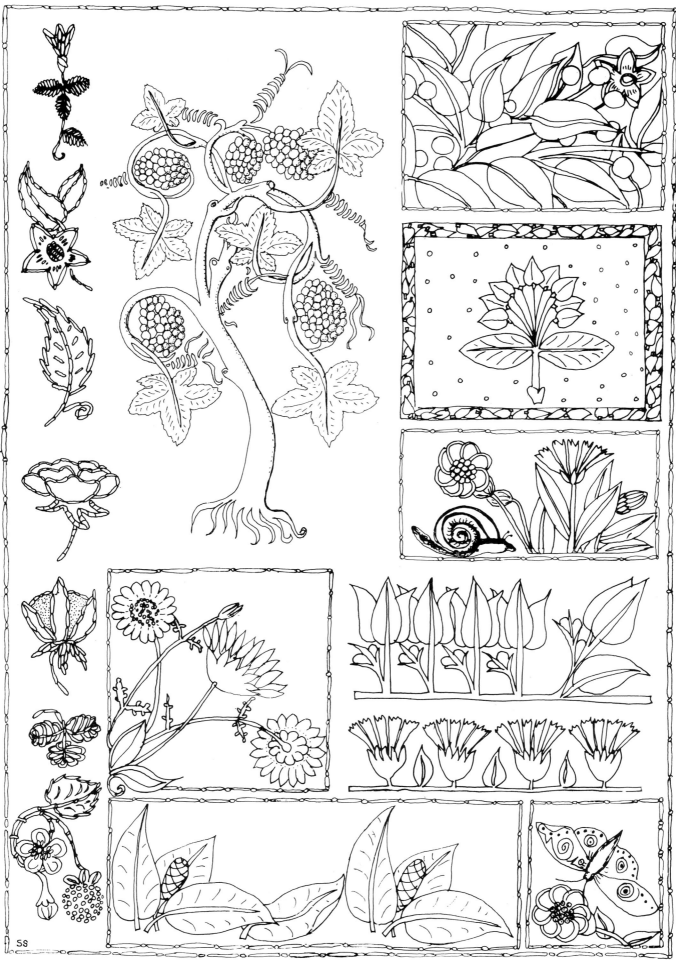

SS

gradually, develop an eye for scale and composition, for the relationship between the structural elements – walls, terraces, paths; the decorative elements – vases, statues, fountains; and the living plants. All this will help enormously in planning and working your designs.

I suggest you keep two notebooks: a small compact one for garden visits with detachable pages for sketches, and a larger garden embroidery album in which to keep photographs, postcards, sketches, pictures from magazines and catalogues, notes on your own garden and samples of threads and fabrics you would like to use. Do try to record, and therefore present, this material as pleasingly as possible even though (or especially because) the notebooks are kept for your own use and only secondly, if at all, for other people.

Gardening and embroidery are arts of arrangement and the pages of your album may spark off new ideas as well as evoke memories of idyllic summer afternoons, of your own garden at its freshest in May or its most poignant in late October. They are exactly what you need to have before you in winter when you may find time to work on a project. I am on my third such album now, and I find it invaluable, not only as a source of ideas for my needlework, but for my garden too. Some pages record plants seen at shows or garden centres, others juxtapose photographs, sketches, a length of striped silk thread from a fishing shop (meant for tying flies but ideal for fly-stitch stems) or a pressed flower from a plant in a friend's garden which I am tempted to embroider or try out in my own.

Last summer I pressed flower heads and complete plants, singly and in groups, to see how useful they might be as a source of designs, and was enthralled both with the process and with the results. Particularly if you find drawing difficult, this is a most satisfying way of getting to know plants intimately and finding out which ones make good subjects for embroidery. In pressing you reduce the flowers from three to two dimensions and, though they lose their brilliance, the muted tones that remain are exceptionally subtle and lovely. In selecting the flowers for pressing you will study them in the hand, and in the process develop a good 'flower eye', noting their structure and removing some leaves and buds, so that when you move them round on a sheet of handmade paper – not an extravagance, but because of its texture as essential as using a sympathetic ground in embroidery – they almost automatically build up into patterns.

You can learn so much from books, classes and garden visits, but gardening and embroidery are practical as well as

'Monet's Garden' by Yvonne Morton. This picture is worked on scrim using a variety of threads and torn strips of material for the willow and wisteria foliage, and wrapped threads for the tree trunk. The path is pink suede lightly quilted.

creative activities. You will learn most of all from the intimate handling of plants, weeding, pruning, pausing to examine the texture and shape of a leaf and noting others that would associate well with it, all of which has its counterpart in embroidery in handling and using materials, trying one thread against another, preparing the ground and working a few stitches upon it. I have wondered many times if there is an embroidery equivalent to the term 'green fingers'. 'Nimble fingers' suggests technical expertise, but this does not mean your embroidery will flourish; it lacks the essential ingredients of love and intuitive understanding implicit in the former term.

Let Russell Page have the last word:

If you wish to make anything grow you must understand it, and understand it in a very real sense. "Green fingers" are a fact, and a mystery only to the unpractised. But green fingers are the extensions of a verdant heart. A good garden cannot be made by somebody who has not developed the capacity to know and love growing things.

'Garden Notes' by Jane Lemon. Album bound in dark-green suede with raised letters, some of which frame tiny painted garden views. Inside are photographs and drawings of plants, paths, walls and fences – information and inspiration for future garden embroidery.

Design by Marian Kratochwil, based on an Elizabethan long cushion in the Victoria and Albert Museum.

CHOOSING A SUBJECT

The scope for garden embroidery is so wide that choosing a subject you will enjoy working is not as simple as it might first appear. Often the choice will be an instinctive one—some colour harmony, the textures of leaves in a tapestry hedge, the shapes of topiary figures silhouetted in a way you had never noticed before, something of this kind will attract your attention, making you reach for your pencil or your camera, or possibly determine you to get a few threads, material and a needle together then and there. Your 'sketch', your 'impression' will have been made, and will then be at hand for future use.

Bonnard was talking about painting when he said, 'The thing must start with a vision, with a moment of excitement. After that you must study the model.' It is just the same in embroidery. After the initial excitement, you must study the subject to determine how best to transpose it into stitches rather than paint. A group of embroiderers visiting Great Dixter near Northiam in East Sussex may gasp at the magical effects of light on the plumage of the topiary birds; but then, and sooner rather than later, each must get to grips with the subject, alone, one embroiderer at work on a chosen subject.

Some garden subjects attract because you immediately see them in terms of stitches, and know they will transpose perfectly. A gravel path suggests closely worked French knots, while a grassy path or lawn may suggest velvet stitch. The gentle contours of the landscape garden suggest quilting, and the regular or random shapes of paving could be matched in patchwork. If you like working on canvas you may find the undulations of gold and yellow in the autumn border turning to freely worked Florentine patterns before your eyes.

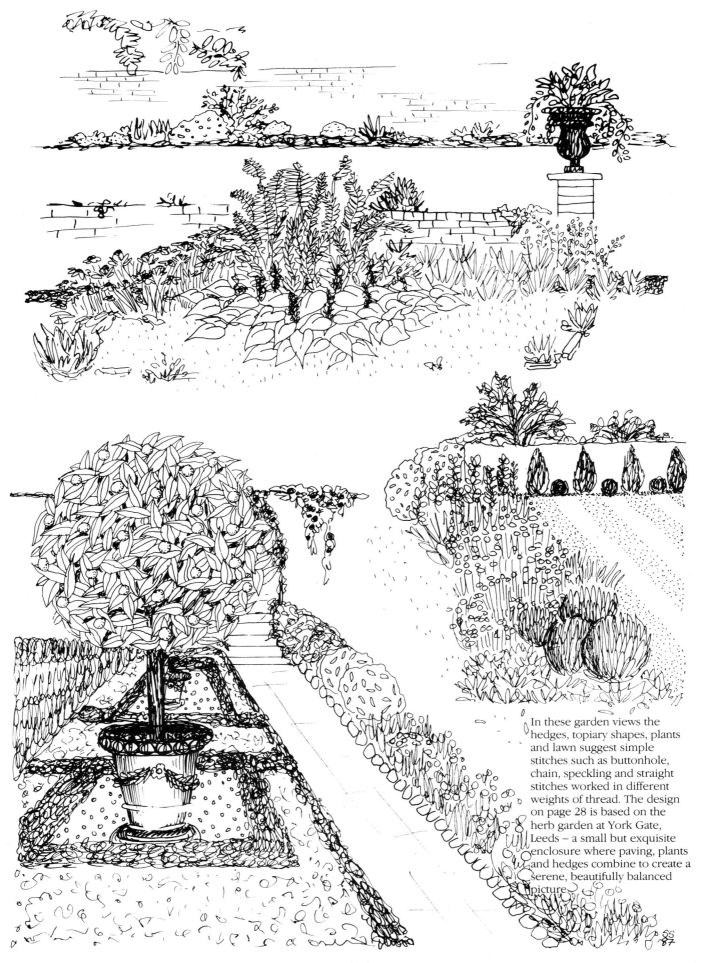

In these garden views the
hedges, topiary shapes, plants
and lawn suggest simple
stitches such as buttonhole,
chain, speckling and straight
stitches worked in different
weights of thread. The design
on page 28 is based on the
herb garden at York Gate,
Leeds – a small but exquisite
enclosure where paving, plants
and hedges combine to create a
serene, beautifully balanced
picture.

A section of 'Trellis', an
exquisite hanging by Grace
Christie worked on handwoven
linen in a great variety of
stitches including interlacing,
buttonhole laid and couched
work. This is 'a beautiful
treatment . . . for owing to the
silk not being cut up into
minute lengths by stitches, its
smooth glossy texture is shown
to full advantage' as you can see
in the shaded and patterned
wings of the butterflies. The
wide border is particularly
beautiful and ingenious in the
corner treatment.

30

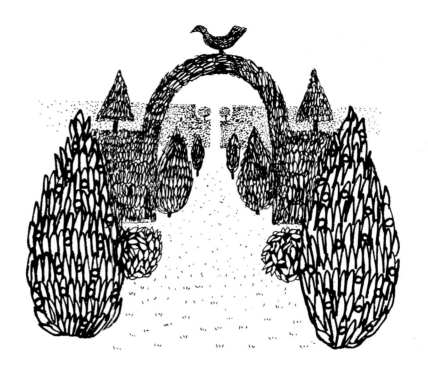

'Topiary Gardens at Great Dixter' by Brenda Murphy inspired by the shapes of topiary birds and clipped hedges in various parts of the garden. Machine embroidery and trapunto quilting on dyed and painted silk. Rainbow applied with bondaweb.

Blackwork garden sampler incorporating some of the spiky symbols used for trees, plants and espaliered fruit trees in Paul Klee's paintings (below), and a sampler based on motifs from old garden books and herbals, decoratively arranged to try out simple stitches (opposite).

Though I do not wish to claim the superiority of embroidery over painting – that would be silly – it remains nonetheless a challenging and exciting truth that stitches are more versatile than the marks a painter can make with a brush. Stitches add a further dimension to your palette, enabling you to convey the textural variety and tactile pleasures of the garden in a unique way. Grace Christie, author of that best of all handbooks of the embroiderer's art, *Samplers and Stitches* (1920), wrote that the 'techniques of embroidery, rather than being disguised need emphasizing – stitches apart from what they express, possess qualities such as beauty of form, ingenuity and mystery, for they are curiously wrought and this is their charm'. The wealth of stitches used in her 'Trellis' hanging are an inspiration in themselves, and are even more remarkable if you study them with a sprig or picture of the real plant before you. Each stitch has been chosen to render a particular quality of the leaf, petal, stem or butterfly's wing, and the exquisite technique using floss and twisted silk emphasizes these qualities still further. Silk is one of the most pleasurable threads to use in garden embroidery, partly because of its softness which invites the touch, just as in the real garden certain plants compel you to reach out and stroke them, and partly because of its quasi-magical way of reflecting light. In the real garden we are delighted by the constant changes of light and shade on foliage, grass and water, and threads with light-reflecting properties help to capture these subtle and fleeting effects. Silk can be used to highlight wool, and by varying the direction of flat stitches such as satin and gobelin, stranded cottons and wools can look remarkably lustrous.

Your choice of subject will be influenced by your taste, the time and materials you have available and your experience both of gardens and embroidery. It is as unwise in embroidery as in the garden to embark on projects that are too time-consuming to be pleasurable, and which end up as a chore or have to be abandoned altogether. Herb gardens make an interesting example. Suppose it is early summer and you have just seen a herb garden of enchantment, scented, well tended, with soft colours and fine foliage combining in a visual feast. Should you establish one in your own garden, or should you embroider it? The ideas are equally seductive. Or could you perhaps begin on both projects at once, charting the progress of the one in the other? Whichever you opt for, the most rigorous planning and selection of plants is necessary to avoid a muddle, part

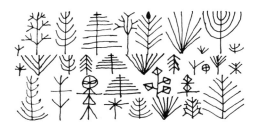

overgrown, part skimpy, lopsided and unlovely.

To avoid this happening you need to begin with a clear idea of the garden's purpose, for only then can you work out what scale and materials would be appropriate. For example – to ask just one of many decisive questions – is the embroidered herb garden to be useful or ornamental? A cushion for an everyday chair would need to be worked in a method and materials capable of withstanding wear, whereas a bed cushion could be shadow quilted in the flimsiest silks in keeping with the character of the room. The ever-practical Miss Jekyll was clearly concerned about this when she was designing and embroidering satin coverings for chairs for Lord Leighton, who much admired her work. 'When I pointed out that the delicate embroidery in coloured silks was not suited to bearing the usual treatment of a chair seat, he gave me the comforting answer, "Never mind, nothing but my eye will ever sit on those chairs".'

I have wondered how Gertrude Jekyll's interest in embroidery began. Born in 1843, she would have learned needlework with her governess, and as a young woman she must have studied the stitches and patterns in the embroideries she bought on her travels in the Levant. As late as 1920 when her sight was very poor she was still experimenting, trying out felt appliqué in a picture of a potted auricula and strawberries which, unlike most of her needlework, has survived until today.

You may feel you need to experiment, to try out methods and materials before committing yourself to a particular project. A most satisfactory way of doing this and exploring the possibilities of garden embroidery in the process, would be to take as your model the working garden described by Russell Page in *The Education of a Gardener*, which though indubitably a garden resembles in every particular a beautiful, highly personal sampler. It was to occupy a rectangular space adjoining his workroom, and was to be designed like a black japanned box of watercolours, with

the overall area divided into small beds separated by paths reminiscent of a botanic garden. He wrote:

> I shall use this garden as paint box, palette and canvas, and in it I shall try out plants for their flower colour, texture of foliage and habit of growth. In some beds I shall set out seedlings for selection, in others bulbs, in others plants for essays in colour. Each bed will be autonomous, its own small world in which the plants will teach me more about their aesthetic possibilities . . . I may hollow out a square or two as pools for water lilies or *Iris kaempferi*.

It was to be a 'trial ground from which I shall always learn', a palette which would change with the seasons and the weather, and in it he would find 'living and growing, the coloured expansions of my pleasures as a painter and gardener'.

If you were to make a sampler following these guidelines, you would, I am sure, find it just as pleasurable and stimulating. The crisscross of paths would establish a grid separating the beds with their diverse treatments, but would also ensure that the overall effect was ordered and coherent. Here you could work out equivalents in stitches and threads for the shapes and textures of the garden, and experiment with colour and tone. The grid would be simple to set out on any evenweave material – canvas would be ideal for experimenting with threads of different weights and with ribbons, cords and raffia as well as wools, silk and cottons. The paths could be left unstitched, painted or filled with paving patterns (see Chapter 12). You might prefer to use a finer ground and experiment with blackwork fillings, or with pulled and white work. Alternatively you could mark the grid on calico and spray, dye or paint the beds and paths (possibly quilting them) and try out machine and free stitchery in the different sections.

As in the real garden the permutations are endless, and whichever methods you choose the sampler will inevitably sharpen your powers of observation and will make you look as you never looked before at the way plants grow, the shape and texture of leaves, buds, stems and flowers, and at the surface qualities of stone, cobbles and brick in the paths. As you work you will be developing the embroiderer's equivalent of 'green fingers', familiarizing yourself 'at least as much through the hands as through the heart' as Russell Page put it 'with the ways and nature of plants and stone, of water and soil'.

As you think out the stitches and decide on the threads

there will be a constant cross-fertilisation between sampler and garden, enabling you little by little to work out subtler plant associations and colour schemes. Like the working garden on which it was based, such a sampler would be a thing of delight in itself and an inspiration for further creation. Each carefully thought out bed might suggest a subject for a further project, where you could develop the ideas within it on a larger scale.

You might now feel ready to embark on a trough garden of miniature bulbs, a bed in a single-colour garden, a pond or water garden. From the sampler you will have learned the importance of concentrating on one idea at a time and developing it as far as it can go. 'The most frequent fault whether in composition or colour is to try to crowd too much into the picture; the simpler effect obtained by means of temperate and wise restraint is always more telling.' Miss Jekyll's advice should be taken to heart by embroiderers, as this disciplined approach is as much the secret of good embroidery as of good gardens.

Take for example the chequerboard garden at Port Lympne in Kent, one of the few great twentieth-century gardens and one which exemplifies this directness and simplicity. It is laid out in alternating squares of grass and flowers in contrasting colours, tulips in spring, begonias in summer. Seen from the balcony of the house it really does resemble a carpet, and this effect must have been all the more striking when it was first laid out in the 1920s. Then, the flower squares were set lower than the grass so that the surface of the chequerboard was perfectly smooth. In embroidery you might concentrate on the intensity of the colour contrast, working out innumerable different tones of each colour in the squares (on canvas, rice and flat stitches might be chosen); or you might try to capture the smoothness of the surface; or, if you made the present planting your model, the contrast between the texture and level of the grass and flowers, using raised chain band for the flowers and tent stitch for the grass. You could bring out the abstract pattern of the chequerboard, or render it realistically with velvet stitch and tiny needle-lace flowers.

The view from the balcony with its decorative ironwork is tempting too, but if you chose this you would have to decide whether to make the chequerboard recede in perspective or to treat it as part of a richly patterned background as in a Persian miniature. Which viewpoint to choose is a crucial and fascinating question in garden embroidery and must accordingly have a chapter to itself.

'Plant sampler' by Penelope Tacey, based on studies of hanging, water and tropical plants. Each section has a cotton perlé satin-stitch border which is continued in finer threads and gold towards the edges of the panel to form a framework for the skilfully blended free and traditional canvas stitches worked in cotton, wool, silk, tape and raffia. Some leaves are in bondaweb techniques with the stems of the vine in handmade cord and the begonia leaves in Suffolk puffs. The outer border was sprayed with car-spray paint overlaid with shot organza.

opposite 'Palette garden sampler' by Dalia Hartman. Canvaswork panel inspired by the description of Russell Page's working garden and stitched as an experiment in mixing flower colour working out from the central red, yellow and blue primary colours to blends of green, orange and purple in the outer beds. Stitches include St John's star, rice, reversed cross and mosaic.

Detail of a herb garden by Sylvia Bramley with marigolds in eyelets, lavender in French knots and the trees surrounding the garden in looped running stitch in fine wool.

Planting begonias in the beds
of the chequerboard at Port
Lympne. This garden was
designed by Russell Page.
Sarah Siddall's drawings show
the garden from above, in
perspective, and partly framed
in the decorative ironwork of
the balcony of the house which
can be seen in the foreground
of the photograph.

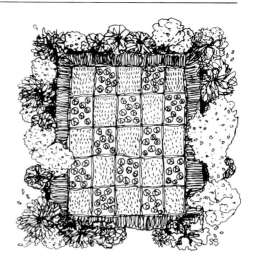

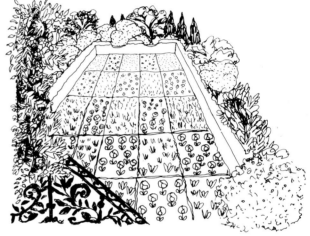

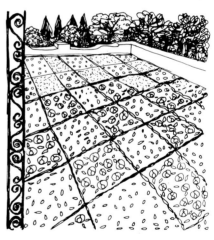

CHOOSING
A VIEWPOINT

Garden designing begins with the making of a flat pattern, in which you may work out the ground plan and thus establish the outer boundary and inner divisions. These include hard materials – stone in terraces, steps, paving – and water in streams, pools and fountains; and living materials, in lawns, trees and borders of flowers. The complex multi-dimensional reality of the garden is thus reduced to flat shapes enabling the designer to concentrate on balancing the various elements harmoniously. The success of any garden, formal or informal, depends on its underlying structure. If the plan is well thought out and in harmony with the house and its setting, the garden should please owner and visitor alike; if not it will be somehow unsatisfactory or even a downright muddle.

By simplifying and formalising the reality of the garden, a plan enables you to look at the garden in a particular schematic way as a plain surface capable of infinite variations in terms of shape, colour and texture. Even if you were up in a balloon looking down on a smallish garden your eyes would still not be able to take in the design as clearly as they can on a plan, but if, in your embroidery, you transfer the plan to your chosen ground, you can work in the shapes and enjoy the garden patterns and texture in a uniquely satisfying way.

'The Mole's Garden' by Susan Smith. The name of this garden finely worked in cottons on linen refers to the chapter heading in the *Wind in the Willows* and to the name of the owner, as the legend Dulce Domum (sweet home) incorporates the letters M-O-L-E. It lovingly records the striped lawn, onion bed, terrace and pots of the real garden.

'Summer Garden' by Vicky Lugg. This panel shows how well a simple plan works as an embroidery pattern. The paved terrace was printed with a small square block using fabric paints. The stripes on the lawn were made by first spraying the lawn area in diluted fabric paint and then respraying with alternate stripes masked with tape. The surrounding border is worked freely with snippets of fabric held down by stars and small detached stitches.

Simple garden plans can easily be adapted as needlework patterns.

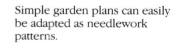

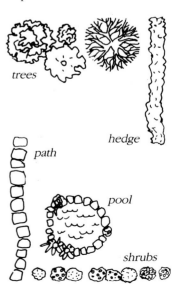

trees

hedge

path

pool

shrubs

Plan of a sunk garden with yew hedges from *Garden Craft Old and New* by John Sedding (1901). The central square could be used as a cushion design.

opposite An abstract design for a canteen garden at Penguin Books designed by John Brookes and inspired by Mondrian's painting.

Perspective view of the same garden.

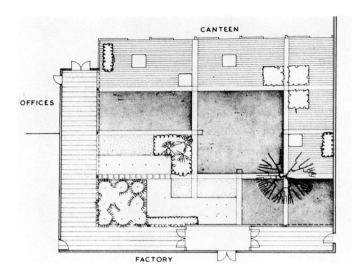

Some garden plans, like the Port Lympne chequerboard, Russell Page's palette garden, and the knots in Chapter 5 are instantly interchangeable with embroidery designs, while others can be easily adapted. You have only to compare the plan and perspective views of the same garden from John Sedding's *Garden Craft Old and New* (1901) to see how well the simple outline of the plan would work as an embroidery pattern. If you wanted a design for a square cushion you could use either the central section or the whole plan, with the curved beds at the far side replaced by rectangular ones to make the design symmetrical. This is a strictly formal design, but informal plans can be just as exciting to develop in embroidery. Some of the most innovative gardens this century have been inspired by modern paintings whose abstract shapes and strong rhythms are transposed into pools, paving, grass and plants. The brilliant Brazilian designer Burle Marx filled the free-flowing shapes on his plans with mosaic paving, dramatic foliage plants and water to create stimulating contrasts and harmonies of colour. In England the Spanish painter Joan Miró inspired Geoffrey Jellicoe's design of interlocked circular stepping stones in the water garden at Sutton Place near Guildford, and this great twentieth-century designer was also much influenced by his friend Ben Nicholson's white reliefs of the thirties. If you made this kind of garden the basis of an embroidery design you could work the shapes in appliqué, patchwork

or quilting. Shadow quilting using several layers of semi-transparent material would be effective.

Since gardens and embroidery are such highly personal arts, your own garden plan may well be the most fascinating and rewarding of all to transpose into embroidery. If you do not have a plan, you must make one. There is no mystique about this; clear instructions are given in garden manuals (see Bibliography), and provided you have a willing helper and a long measuring tape it is not difficult to make a rapid sketch plan in the garden, noting as many measurements as possible to establish the boundaries of terraces, beds, paths and other features. You may feel your garden is somehow missing its potential, in which case your embroidery project may well provide the very impetus to get to grips with the design of the real garden at the same time. The measurements of the sketch are transferred to graph or squared paper, providing a grid which can double as an embroidery design. If you want to modify the plan, place tracing paper over the outline and then consider how you can improve the relationship between the 'hard' and planted areas, the siting of the features, the spacing of trees, large shrubs and so on. Get together some sheets of coloured paper (tissue paper is ideal) in blue, green, brown and grey to indicate areas of water, lawn, planting, terraces and paths, and cut or tear them into the shapes on your plan; move them about, making alterations, and gradually a new pattern will evolve.

Drawings of the Rose Garden at Cliveden by Geoffrey Jellicoe. The static formal design was replaced by the freer treatment on the right whose rhythms resemble an abstract painting. This kind of design suggests appliqué or shadow quilting using layers of semi-transparent material or possibly handmade paper or felt.

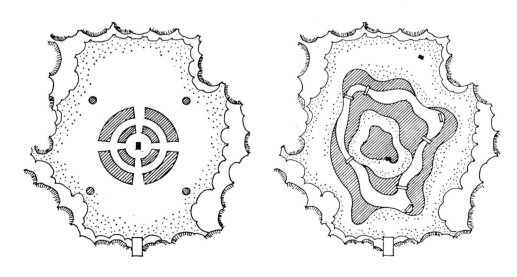

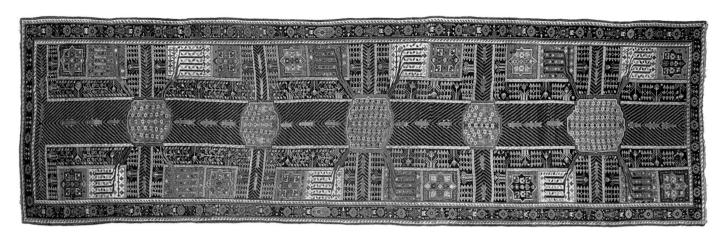

Late eighteenth-century Persian garden carpet based on the layout of a water garden.

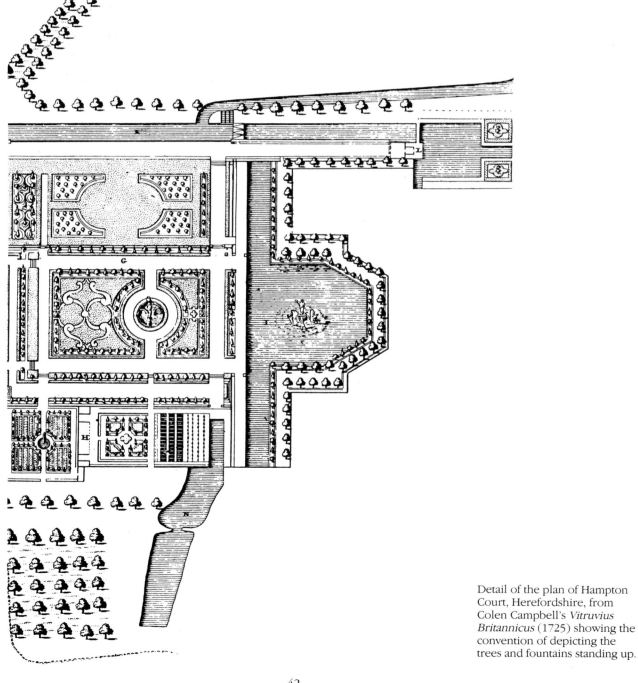

Detail of the plan of Hampton Court, Herefordshire, from Colen Campbell's *Vitruvius Britannicus* (1725) showing the convention of depicting the trees and fountains standing up.

'Campion Garden' by Margaret Rochester inspired by memories of Hampton Court near London and the phrase 'all is work and nowhere space' describing an Elizabethan garden in a poem by Thomas Campion. The ground plan was transferred to evenweave and tent stitched in wool, then the plants and garden features, seen in profile, were added in stranded cotton.

The neat rectangular beds of the garden contrast with the random shape of the fields in this naïve pictorial plan from John Worlidge's *Systema Agriculturae* of 1668.

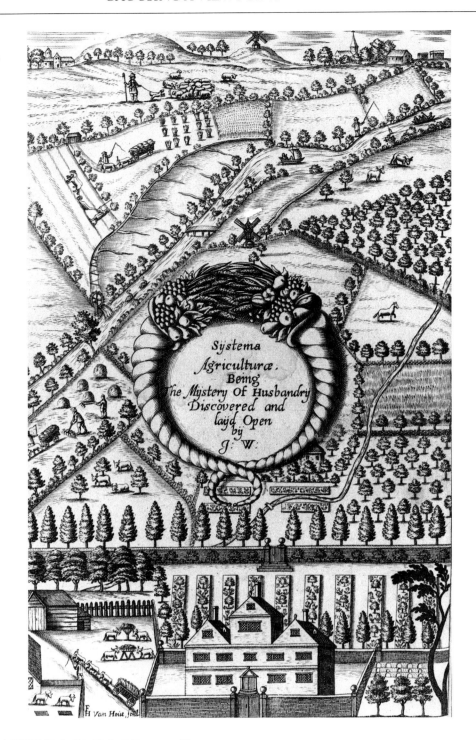

Gardeners at work in two woodcuts from a late (1651) edition of Thomas Hill's *The Gardener's Labyrinth*.

However natural you want your garden to look, the various elements must still be carefully balanced and in proportion one to another. This supposes a strong geometric basis rather than the unconnected shapes and vague serpentine meanderings which characterise all too many gardens of the 'island bed' school – which has its counterpart in some anaemic-looking designs of the fifties and sixties in embroidery.

In plans, vertical features like trees are generally indicated as circles, but sometimes a convention is followed where trees, fountains and even small ornamental buildings are shown standing up. This is a characteristic of pictorial plans which ingeniously represent the garden from two or even more angles at the same time, often with naïve but charming results which transpose happily in embroidery. One of the earliest known pictures of a garden is a pictorial plan in the British Museum. It is an ancient Egyptian water garden, with a lotus pool edged by a papyrus border, and shaded on all sides by fruit trees drawn from different angles, with the birds and fish in the pool seen in profile – a favourite convention in Egyptian art. The plan is accurate enough for us to reconstruct the garden, yet it is the pictorial treatment which brings this information alive, vividly suggesting the atmosphere of seclusion and repose in the original garden created four thousand years ago. Here picture and pattern combine decoratively and expressively; Walter Crane saw its potential as an embroidery design, describing it as 'a very pretty piece of ornament and would embroider well as a tablecloth centre'. Just how effective this kind of treatment can be in embroidery can be seen in Belinda Pollit's cross-stitch cushion on page 47 based on a simple four-square plot, enclosed by trees flattened out into a decorative border. Several small rabbits introduce a pictorial note, adding considerably to the cushion's liveliness and charm.

It is interesting to compare the flat pattern of the ancient Egyptian garden with the wonderful garden carpets woven in Persia in the sixteenth and seventeenth centuries. Here decoratively patterned channels of water divide the garden into a network of flowery plots set between long borders of shrubs and trees ingeniously flattened out to suggest their structure over the corner beds. Some of the plants are seen from above, others are in profile, as are the fish swimming in the channels. Together water, trees and flowers combine to create an enthrallingly rich and varied surface. The carpets were often taken out into the garden for parties and in Persian miniature paintings they can frequently be seen depicted in square and rectangular shapes rather than in perspective.

Two crude woodcuts from *The Gardener's Labyrinth* (1651) show very well how an artist has chosen to use, or not to use, perspective in different parts of the picture. In the first woodcut the irrigation channels of a small square garden are being filled with water from a 'great Squirt' by a gardener standing beside the flat pattern of the water channels in the centre of which a single flower sprouts up as jauntily as those depicted in the second scene, where an attempt has been made to represent the beds, but not the tools, in perspective. Both woodcuts could be described as pictorial plans, and either could serve in embroidery as the starting point for a flat pattern, or a picture, or a combination of the two.

Pictorial plan of an English Garden from *Jardins Anglo Chinois* (1776–88) by G. L. Le Rouge.

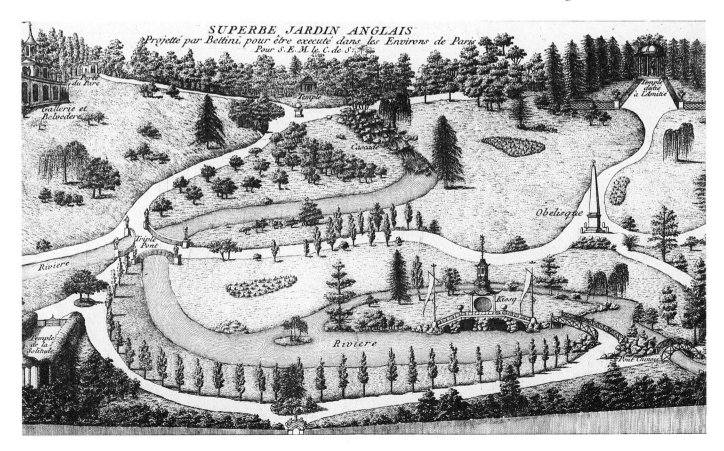

Whether you introduce perspective into your garden embroidery, the use you make of it, and the extent to which you make it convincing is entirely a matter of taste. But if you incline more towards 'picture-making' than 'pattern-making', some knowledge of how it works is desirable. Perspective is an illusionary device, used in picture making to lead the eye into what is still in fact a flat surface. It is a way of representing the world around us based on a particular set of conventions. In Sedding's picture on page 40, perspective is used to give an illusion of depth, drawing your eye into the garden. The picture on the page is flat, but the trees, hedges, walls and pots are made to look solid by the use of shading and cast shadows. The picture represents the garden viewed from one point, so that the parallel lines of walls and beds and hedges recede into the distance and appear to meet at a vanishing point on the horizon, as you can verify if you lay a pencil along the paths.

In the garden the principle is easily understood if you look at any picture of a lawn cut with a mower which produces 'stripes'. The stripes become narrower the further away they are. To depict the relative distance of the trees, hedges and so on from your eye these objects too are made to diminish in size as the distance increases.

The appearance of the garden will change dramatically if the viewpoint is altered. To test this out, try photographing your own garden or sketching it from as many different viewpoints as possible; from the attic or roof, from the upper windows or balcony, and at ground level from a variety of different angles. Do this at different times of day, and include some close-ups of good plant associations or any feature that pleases your eye. If you now compare these images of your garden with the ground plan, you will be in a much better position to decide which would transpose most effectively into the kind of embroidery you enjoy doing. Try

the tracing-paper method described in Chapter 1, and as your pen follows the outlines of trees, pools and plants you may have the curious impression that you are seeing the garden as if for the first time, exploring its shapes and forms, and seeing how they interlock and make balanced groupings.

If you have no garden of your own, or if you would rather look elsewhere for inspiration, you can gather similar material – sketches, photographs and notes – from some other garden which you particularly admire. The problem remains the same: how to begin? and which viewpoint do you choose?

Suppose you were to visit Sissinghurst in Kent in late spring to make notes for an embroidery based on the celebrated White Garden. Armed with the guide which contains the ground plan, you would do well to begin by climbing the Tower which stands high in the centre of the gardens. Walk round the parapet seeing, from high above, each part of the scheme. From this viewpoint you can appreciate the beauty of the whole design with its skilfully planned and linked compartments, and you can see how the strictly formal plan is softened by the informal profusion of the planting which echoes the natural abundance of the Kentish countryside roundabout, with its farms, fields, orchards and woodland. The gardens are different from, but in complete harmony with, the surrounding rural landscape, and the avenues of poplars link the two together, leading your eye out into the meadows and woods. From the Tower you have a series of bird's-eye views including one of the White Garden with its geometrical layout of box-edged beds, straight paths and the billowy shape of the silvery willow-leaved pear casting its gentle shade on the statue beneath. At the centre is the green canopy of the white rose, *Rosa longicuspis*, trained over a metal frame,

'Garden' by Verina Warren. In this embroidered picture, perspective engages the eye and draws it into the garden. Note how sunlight catches the foliage of trees and hedges and how well the painted mount complements and extends the embroidery.

'Rabbit'; cushion by Belinda Pollit worked entirely in cross stitch, with the four-square plot surrounded by a 'frame' of trees.

Wall fresco of an Egyptian water garden.

Tree peony and libertia by the gate in the White Garden.

and in all the beds around you can admire the subtle textural and tonal variety of the planting.

When you come down from the Tower and, at ground level, enter the White Garden, its design is not so wholly apparent. Nevertheless, as you walk among the beds, the straight box edgings and the patterns of the brick and stone paths always guide your eye to the focal points of the now visible statue of Rosandic's virgin crowned by pear foliage and to the great Ming vase under the rose. Walk on to the end of the path, where a wrought-iron gate frames the distant view of the Weald. Beside it the huge papery-white blooms of a tree peony accentuate the fragility of the slender libertia with its butterfly blooms.

Sit down to note the association and your viewpoint changes again. Now you are even more aware of the forms of the plants and the variations in tone and texture. In an article written in 1950 for the *Observer* Vita Sackville-West described how she imagined her grey-green and white garden would look:

Charcoal sketch by Alison Hird of the rose canopy in the White Garden at Sissinghurst, one of many made in preparation for the model on page 51.

When you sit on this seat you will be turning your backs to the yew hedge and from there I hope you will survey a low sea of grey clumps of foliage, pierced here and there by tall white flowers . . . there will be white peonies and white irises with their grey leaves . . . at least I hope there will be all those things. I don't want to boast in advance about my grey, white and green garden. It may be a terrible failure. I wanted only to suggest that such experiments are worth trying, and that you can adapt them to your own taste and your own opportunities.

When she decided to recreate the White Garden in needlework, Alison Hird made innumerable experiments before choosing a viewpoint and deciding on a method. She began by visiting the garden regularly in the late spring and summer, taking photographs of the view from the Tower, and of the willow-leaved pear, rose canopy and plant associations. Fascinated by the possibilities of the changing viewpoint she eventually tried out a wide-angled and fish-eye lens which produced exactly the striking optical effect she needed for the entirely three-dimensional treatment she

'Poppies in the White Garden' and 'The White Garden at Sissinghurst' by Jenny Chippindale were both inspired by the diverse shapes and textures in the garden. The poppies are in finely pleated chiffon with seed heads worked with woven wheels on a ground of pleated and sprayed silk. The White Garden panel is in surface stitchery on a sprayed evenweave ground with the silver pear foliage in cretan stitch, the foxgloves in vandyke and satin stitch and the stachys in raised chain band worked in soft wool. The outline of the tall branching thistle is sprayed through a stencil.

'The White Garden at Sissinghurst' by Alison Hird. Contemporary stumpwork on a polyboard base. The paths are plain felt printed with a potato block to simulate bricks, with larger paving stones cut out and applied. The yew hedges are handmade and dyed felt, ingeniously strengthened with green scouring pad, and the same felt, its surface enlivened with cardings and snippets of yarn, forms the foliage of the silver pear and white rose. The roses are French knots and the canopy frame is wool-covered wire. The gate also has a wire frame with the ironwork pattern in running stitch and couching on black net. All the threads were dyed to match the subtle tones in the real garden, with the 'hummock' plants worked spirally in crochet and applied or made as pompoms. Machine tufting on calico suggests ornamental grasses, and the verbascum leaves are leather sprayed with paint.

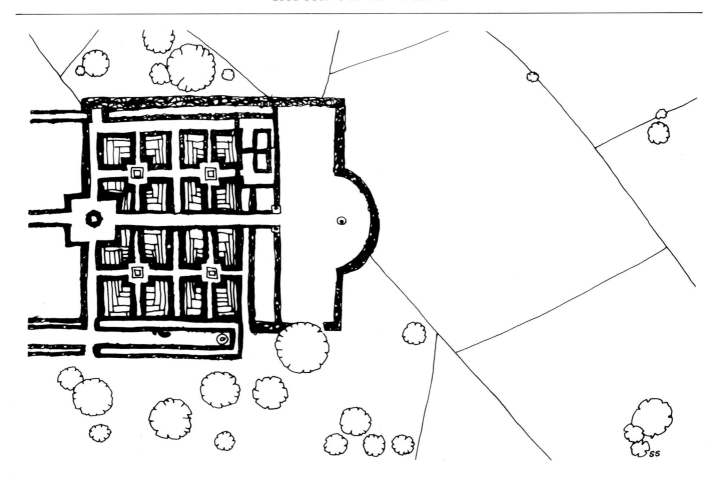

Patchwork design based on the plan of Sissinghurst in the guide book, showing how the regular beds in the White Garden might be adapted in log cabin and the surrounding fields in random shapes.

The archway in the White Garden.

felt would best convey her excitement and pleasure in the planting. Using her notes, photographs, drawings and the plan of the garden in the guide book she evolved a card model which she painted and 'planted' with tiny fronds of foliage. This in its turn was photographed to check that the novel viewpoint would work. Her garden is designed to hang vertically on the wall and to give the impression that the viewer is approaching the rose canopy at the centre. The flowers and foliage were made individually, with an ingenuity that rivals the seventeenth-century raised work which in part inspired the piece. Many of the plants are secured to the base by pins with the delightful effect that they can be moved about – a practical solution that would surely have appealed to Vita Sackville-West with her liking for stumpwork. Indeed in an article *A Sense of Colour*, she describes how she would pick long flower stems and move them from one part of the garden to another 'sticking them into the ground and then standing back to admire the harmony . . . putting in a dash of colour here, taking out another dash there, until the whole composition is to one's liking, and at least one knows exactly what effect will be produced twelve months hence'.

The opportunities for embroidery inspired by the gardens at Sissinghurst are tantalising. You might find the bird's-eye view with the contrast between the formal layout and the natural countryside the most appealing. It has become a cliché to describe irregularly shaped fields as 'patchwork', but here surely is a method you could experiment with. The random shapes of the fields and woods could be worked in crazy patchwork or inlay as a frame to the more complex geometric patterns which would render the garden. A late eighteenth-century shell pattern patchwork hanging in the Victoria and Albert Museum has a diamond pattern applied over it in green ruched ribbon, an idea which might be elaborated here to enhance the formality of the box-edged compartments. The treatment could be entirely flat, or you could try to express your pleasure looking down into the secret enclosures by working them in a patchwork pattern with a three-dimensional effect like log cabin. Tiny hexagons, squares or diamonds could be assembled to suggest drifts of plants melting into one another. Dyeing the fabric first would provide you with a wide enough range of tones for this kind of treatment, or you might try minutely patterned fabrics further varied by surface stitchery, or use different fabrics

such as velvet and fine wool to bring out the textural contrasts. You would need to choose fabrics of similar weight for ease of handling, and consider whether the work would have to be cleaned at a later date, in which case prewashed cottons with the dye properly set would be the most suitable.

You might prefer to base your design on the ground plan of the White Garden, which could easily be enlarged by photocopy to fit your chosen ground. Canvas would be an obvious choice, but a 'white garden' might suggest whitework with needlepoint or counted thread fillings to suggest the density of the planting, remembering that Vita Sackville-West preferred 'exaggeration; big groups, big masses'. She wrote: 'I am sure that it is more effective to plant twelve tulips together than to split them into two groups of six.' Her own description of the White Garden as 'a sea of grey clumps of foliage' also suggests an interpretation in quilting, either in monochrome with wadding and cording to establish the layout, or shadow quilting to bring out the subtle variations of green and white, using tiny snippets of fabric and thread caught in drifts between the muslin backing and a semi-transparent top layer of organza or silk.

Your photographs and sketches may suggest a pictorial treatment. Gertrude Jekyll would have thought this desirable for she wrote: 'One of the objects of a good garden is that it shall be pictorially beautiful – that it shall be a series of enjoyable pictures painted with living flowers.' One sure test of a good garden is that it does indeed present a series of beautifully composed and well balanced pictures, each leading to another and leading you on to explore and delight in what you find. But let Miss Jekyll continue: 'One wants one beautiful picture at a time, not a muddle of means and materials that properly sorted and disposed might compose a dozen. I do not say that it is easy, on the contrary it wants a good deal of knowledge that only comes with labour and effort.'

Your picture of the White Garden at Sissinghurst might represent the statue beneath the willow-leaved pear, the Ming vase surrounded by pots of sweet-scented geraniums, a drift of poppies or columbines. But I suspect that one or more of your photographs or sketches will show the garden framed by the brick archway, the wrought-iron gate or the openings in the yew hedge which enhance the view, just as a fine picture is enhanced by a beautiful and appropriate frame.

4

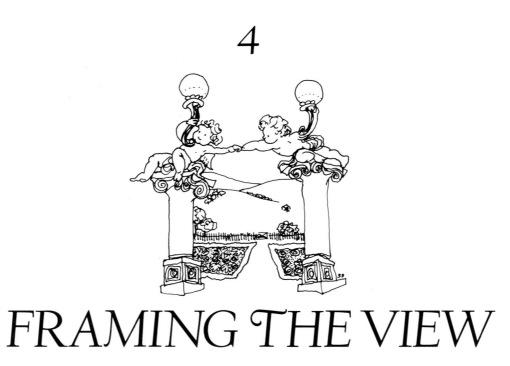

FRAMING THE VIEW

'In every situation a beyond implies discovery and affects the imagination.'

The Art and Practice of Landscape Gardening,
Ernest Milner (1890)

Many of the most exciting and inspiring gardens are those with multiple compartments. Imagine yourself exploring such a garden. Ahead of you there is an arched opening in the wall and through it you can glimpse a fountain or a solitary statue in the next enclosure. The arch frames the view and draws you irresistibly towards it to see more of what lies beyond. Good garden designers use framing devices of all kinds – arches, gates, gateways and apertures in walls and hedges – to direct your steps and make you see the garden unfold before you in a series of pictures. Some houses and gardens built and laid out in the thirties even incorporated special viewing frames in their design.

Any frame, whether it is a window, a doorway, a gate or an opening in a hedge or wall, controls your view urging you to focus your eye through it, to see what lies beyond. It can

suggest the mood of the garden beyond, making it appear more welcoming, romantic or mysterious from the garden or room where you are now. Its treatment in embroidery is particularly interesting as it can become as important or even more important than the garden it surrounds. You could make the frame and view separately, as if you were designing stage scenery. If you chose an archway as your subject, you could paint or spray the 'backdrop' on calico, silk or cotton, washing the fabric vigorously several times to remove every trace of dressing, and, using drawing pins or a staple gun, stretching it out taut as a drum on a board or old wooden picture frame; it is easiest to get the fabric really tight if it is slightly damp. Paint or spray at once for a misty effect with the colours bleeding into one another; a dry ground will produce more clearly defined outlines.

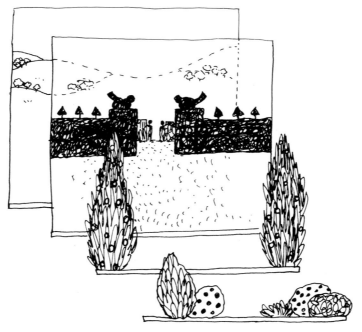

The cones of box and foreground shrubs form a decorative frame using the

'stage scenery' method. These could be machine embroidered on vanishing muslin.

'Walled Garden' by Sue Bakker. Machine embroidery on a painted and sprayed ground. The framing arch is made separately, and the plants are embroidered on vanishing muslin and applied.

The 'stage scenery' method explained in a diagram based on the 'Walled Garden' above. The 'backdrop' is painted and sprayed; the path, shrubs and vase are machine embroidered. The arch is painted calico, and the foreground climbers are machine embroidered on vanishing muslin.

Painting on fabric is different from painting on paper because of the way the colours tend to merge. To begin with it is difficult to judge how far they will spread, but practice will quickly tell you this, and anyway you do not often need to be too precise. If you have a box of water colours or some tubes of gouache or acrylic it is sensible to try these out before investing in special paints or dyes. Begin simply with three broad stripes to represent sky, a hedge and grass using a large brush. You are not trying to make a finished painting but a ground for embroidery, and the enormous advantage of painting or spraying is that you can achieve far greater subtlety of tone than is possible using bought materials. The greens can be varied and intensified by further layers of spraying or by stippling with a small sponge or toothbrush; the sky can be masked with paper while you do this. The fountain jet could be worked directly on the backdrop or on semi-transparent material such as organza placed over it. You could use iridescent threads in running stitch or lines of minute French knots.

To make the framing arch you could again paint, spray or print a brickwork pattern using a simple block. The layers need mounting and stretching carefully to be effective, and you may prefer a single ground, canvas perhaps, with the view finely worked in silk and the brickwork in stranded cotton over two threads.

In Sue Bakker's 'Walled Garden' the archway and view are both on sprayed and painted silk, with machine embroidery worked directly on the backdrop and archway, and on vanishing muslin to create the climbing and foreground plants which are used exactly in the manner of 'flats' in stage scenery. All manner of lacy effects can be created with free machine embroidery on the new disappearing fabrics which dissolve in cold or boiling water, and they lend themselves perfectly to garden subjects. Individual flowers, leaves and entire plants can be made by drawing them out on the fabric firmly secured in an embroidery hoop and then filling the shapes with a network of criss-crossing lines or tiny spirals, making certain that the lines of stitching interlock, otherwise the threads will unravel when the base is dissolved in water. You can create the finest cobweb effects or build up the stitches one on top of each other for a stiffer, denser texture. Because of the danger of shrinking, silk and wool threads are safer on the cold water type of fabric, and whichever you use you must pull the embroidery carefully into shape once the base has dissolved. If you want three-dimensional effects like curled leaves or shaggy petals, take them out of the water a little earlier and mould them into shape while still damp.

If you photographed your garden from your house as suggested in the previous chapter you will doubtless have included a view through a window or doorway. Should you have sash windows, the glazing bars provide a useful grid, and the same applies to diamond or small square-patterned leaded lights. As I look out of my workroom window in London the six lower panes divide the view of my own and my neighbours' walled gardens into six different views complete in themselves of which at least four would make interesting designs. One has a brightly coloured child's swing under a weeping willow, another a small greenhouse and fishpond, yet another a superb golden acacia (*Robinia pseudoacacia* 'Frisia') whose delicate foliage gradually changes from a bright acid green to an ever-astonishing brilliant yellow, reaching its apogée in October when it outshines everything around it. Last year I picked flowers from the garden each month and set them in a vase on a table by the window in order to record in sketches and photographs the changing flowers and backdrop, in its constant framework, with the intention of making a series of small embroideries. They were to be inside-outside garden views, as pleasing to me in February when the garden was covered in snow and the only flowers were three pink camellias in a small Chinese vase, as in May when the fresh spring greenery intensified the mauves, reds and purple of parrot tulips in a tall glass jug.

A window distances you from the garden. The sight of it can be tantalizing in summer when you must work indoors, but comforting in winter when it is too cold to be enjoyable outside. Have you, I wonder, ever visited a country house where parts of the gardens are private but can be glimpsed from the upper windows; are not these the views that most intrigue you and make you long to explore them? Or have you experienced the thrill of arriving on holiday late at night, and in the morning opening the windows onto a garden and landscape new to you and made more inviting – though you are not aware of it at the time – by being seen from a distance in a frame of blue or green shutters reminiscent of a painting by Bonnard or Matisse, frilled muslin curtains, striped blinds or the decorative ironwork of a balcony?

Elaborate window display from E. A. Maling's *Handbook for Ladies* (1870).

'A Peep at a Town Garden' from *Rustic Adornments for Homes of Taste* by Shirley Hibberd (1870) depicts a garden seen from inside a conservatory through a 'frame' of foliage.

'Indoor Garden' by the author. Ochre Honan silk painted with water colour is worked with straight stitches and machine whip stitch. A vase of camellias and three pots containing *Iris danfordiae*, species crocus and an auricula 'more like the inventions of a miniaturist, or a designer of embroidery than a thing which will grow easily and well in a garden' as Vita Sackville-West described this captivating plant, are set on an Indian table by the window as a foretaste of spring.

A window is a potent and mysterious image, and a way of looking at the world which has always attracted artists. Humphry Repton, the great garden designer of the 1800s, considered 'there is no subject connected with landscape gardening of more importance . . . than the window through which the landscape is seen'. In embroidery it can be transposed in many different methods and its strong framework provides a good starting point for a design. It can frame a view of your own garden or one you admire, or be purely imaginary. You may for example combine the decorative framework of a Gothic window with a view of a 'picturesque' garden merging into the surrounding country-side. You could paint or spray your ground using pale misty tones for the distant view, and stronger tones for the garden, with light surface stitchery to indicate trees, a hedge or a tiny pavilion. The foreground would be more detailed and in stronger tones still with flowers growing up from a border below, or a vase on the sill with flowers and a trug basket.

Window and view could be worked on the same piece of fabric, with the frame marked in tacking threads to be finished after the view in simple straight or couched stitches, or you could cut a stencil and colour the view through it leaving the glazing bars plain. Alternatively you could make the frame separately in a non-fraying material like felt or paper. The treatment in Jan Attrill's 'Secret Garden' on page 62 is particularly striking. Here the idea of leaving the glazing bars void came from drawings she had made of condensation misting the outline of the panes and fragmenting the garden view. The shapes were transferred

'Golden Acacia' by the author. Hand and machine embroidery on a silk satin ground painted with water colour. The foliage of the tree is in whip stitch with French knots and speckling stitches in floss and twisted silk. Flowers in the vase include *Saxifraga fortunei* and the purple berries of *Callicarpa giraldiana*.

Window garden from *Domestic Floriculture* by F. W. Burbidge (1874).

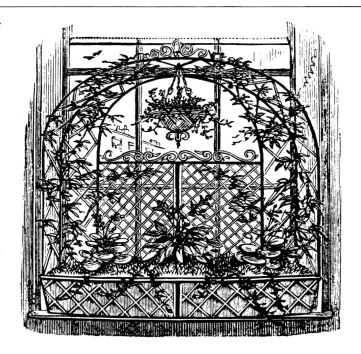

An archway from *How to Lay Out a Garden* by Edward Kemp (1864).

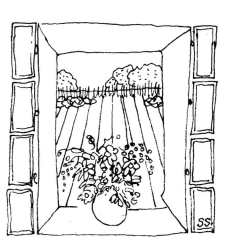

Designs which frame the view through windows and openings in walls and hedges.

A Victorian window garden
with tiny pots and hanging
plants.

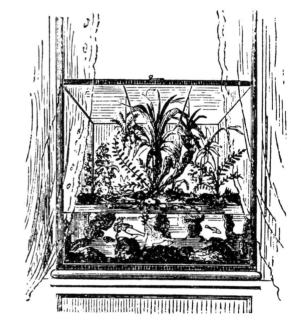

Inside view of an outside
window box and aquarium
combined, from *Domestic
Floriculture*.

'Secret Garden' by Jan Attrill. Canvaswork applied to shot-silk organza. The design, combining real and imaginary elements, is based on a photograph of a wild mysterious garden freely adapted to include delphiniums and moon daisies from the maker's own garden.

to canvas and the sky and flowers worked in tent stitch, after which the canvas was applied to organza and the 'bars' cut away. The colour and thickness of the bars can change the view dramatically. If you experiment, you will find that dark bars intensify the colours in the garden; heavy ones on the other hand emphasize the plane of the window, bringing home to you that the view beyond is genuinely separate, distant, distinct from the room you are in on this side of the window. In this way the most interesting effects of super-imposed patterns can be achieved.

The window itself can become a garden in miniature, an idea that goes back to the sixteenth century when Thomas Tusser suggested that housewives should grow pots of lilies, double marigolds, sweet williams and roses in boxes in their windows. It was taken up again enthusiastically by the Victorians in the most complex ornamental arrangements. Window boxes inside the living room were furnished with decorative tiles, and the whole window could be fitted up with special shelves and provision for hanging plants. The descendants of these window gardens can be seen in the rows of pots arranged on the sill between prettily looped-back curtains, or sometimes in front of drawn net curtains as if for the benefit of the passer-by.

The favourite window plants – geraniums, fuchsias and trailing evergreens – frame or partially screen the garden view, whether they are planted outside in boxes or inside on shelves and sill. This suggests a treatment using embroidery on semi-transparent material or dissolvable fabric, building up two or more layers to give the idea of the relative distances of plants, curtains and the window itself.

Unlike the window which distances you from the view, a doorway invites you to step over the threshold. Here too a dark surround, as in Jenny Chippindale's 'Open Garden Door' on page 67, emphasises the glimpsed freshness and brightness and draws you towards it. The sunlit glimpse of Kew Gardens in Mary Grierson's picture on page 66 is seen through the dark entrance to the extraordinary gallery made to house the brilliant flower paintings of the Victorian artist and explorer Marianne North. Miniature versions of these paintings worked in tent stitch form a glowing frame to the painted view of trees and lawn and exactly catch the spirit of this unique place.

'Dreamed Garden–et in arcadia ego' by Paddy Ramsay. Free machine quilting and appliqué in velvet and satin. The picture is based on Italian Gardens and Cragside in Northumberland and expresses the maker's dream of being in such a garden in preference to her everyday surroundings. The openings in the hedge and sentinel cypresses beyond intensify the mysterious atmosphere of a dream world. The frame is made and painted by Paddy Ramsay to complement the vivid pinks and greens of the rhododendrons.

Gateways also control your view of the garden and provide a further source of decorative and expressive designs. Any gateway implies movement into or out of the garden, or from one part of it to another, and its appearance can also help to enhance the atmosphere of the garden beyond. A solid gate in a high wall is a forbidding image, shutting you out altogether, whereas a half-open gate is just the opposite, letting you glimpse the view beyond and inviting you to explore a hitherto secret place. An openwork gate in wood or iron acts in the same way, hinting that you may peer through it in the hopes of seeing more.

Gates and gateways often bring together different textures which can be interestingly interpreted in embroidery. A simple wooden gate to a cottage garden, with an arch of yew and guardian topiary peacocks, or a delicate wrought-iron gate in a brick wall, overhung with the heart-shaped leaves of the claret vine, suggest innumerable possibilities for transposing the living and hard surfaces. You could bring out the tonal difference between the rich wine reds and purples of the leaves and the faded terracotta of the wall, or the textural contrast between the curious velvety bloom on the leaves and the smoothness of the painted ironwork. The patterns of wrought- and cast-iron gates and gateways are wonderfully varied and exciting to use in garden embroidery, and it is well worth studying examples in museums like the Victoria and Albert in London. Wrought-iron, forged by hand, is more delicate than ironwork cast in a mould whose appearance is robust and often more angular; this is worth noting when transposing the effect in embroidery. A filigree fine wrought-iron gate lets you see more of the garden beyond than a heavy cast-iron one, so heavier threads and a chunkier stitch would be more appropriate. A plain iron gate with vertical bars could be rendered in long straight stitches; or fine wire could be wrapped in silk and couched down, a method which would work well for a simple scrolling pattern. In more elaborate designs with exuberant coiling scrollwork, machine whip or satin stitch would transpose the free-flowing quality of the patterns perfectly. In handwork, stem, split or trailing stitch

Gateways inviting you to explore the garden.

Characteristic grillwork for a circular opening from *Chinese Houses and Gardens* by Henry Inn and S. C. Lee (1940).

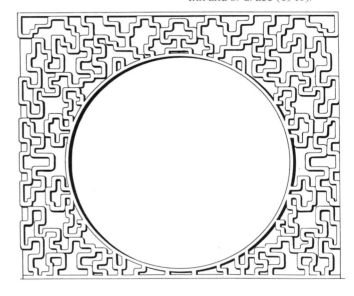

could be tried out. Some of the more geometric repeating patterns closely resemble blackwork and could be worked in running, herringbone, back and satin stitch on hexagonal net, or in darning and looped stitches on square-mesh net which could be cut out and applied, or mounted over the garden backdrop as a separate layer.

For many centuries, special windows and doors have been made in Chinese gardens to frame particularly harmonious views with delicate clay grills in intricate, sometimes symbolic designs such as fans, vases, squares or circles. The filigree effect of windows like these could be interpreted in pulled or drawn thread work either by hand or machine. Frame and view complement each other, and Chinese doors and gates were, like the windows, most carefully designed to lead your eye and your steps towards the garden pictures which could be circular, as in the famous moon gates, or in the shape of huge leaves or four-lobed plum blossom. All formed beautiful frames to the simplest but most refined compositions – a single rock and bamboo, their shadows cast on the white wall behind them.

When from the eighteenth century onwards western architects and garden designers began building Chinese pavilions and using these motifs in English gardens, they were entranced by their decorative appeal, but often failed to understand the complex and serious nature of the garden view beyond. If you are tempted to use them as the basis for a design, be sure to keep the garden view exceedingly simple.

Archway in wood, from Edward Kemp's *How to Lay Out a Garden*, which would transpose well in laid work.

'Terrace Walk and Herb Garden' from Thomas H. Mawson's *Art and Craft of Garden Making* (1900). The central gateway frames the view of the garden beyond and leads your steps towards it.

Pleasing patterns in a gate from *Art and Craft of Garden Making*.

The wrought-iron gateway at Athelhampton in Dorset and the metal arch at Portmeirion in north Wales form decorative frames for the pool garden and flower-filled vase.

'Kew from the Marianne North Gallery' by Mary Grierson. Like Marianne North in her day, Mary Grierson is celebrated for her exquisite botanical illustrations, and was for many years the official artist at the Royal Botanic Gardens at Kew. The view of the gardens on painted silk with light surface stitchery is in complete contrast to the colours and method used for the paintings which form the frame. These echo the Berlin woolwork of Marianne North's time.

opposite 'Open Garden Door' by Jenny Chippindale. Patchwork hanging of the maker's own garden in Kent seen from inside the house. Surface stitchery is added to bring out the forms of lavender, artemisias and alliums with couched stems. The Christmas cactus has been put outside in its pot and geraniums stand by the door.

KNOTS AND KNOT GARDENS

Ever since the Renaissance, embroidery has provided a unique and fascinating record of the changing fashions in gardens. It is therefore no surprise to find the modern gardener's enthusiasm for reinterpreting knots in gardens matched by the embroiderer's pleasure in rediscovering an ideal subject for pattern making and experiments in texture and colour. In both arts the excitement lies in reworking the old designs while using plants and materials unknown to the first makers in an original and personal way. In the garden this means seeking out old varieties and mixing them with flowers and bulbs which will harmonize in texture, shape and colour; in embroidery it means finding a method and stitches to recreate the richness and variety of the living patterns.

Elaborate geometrical knots laid out in thyme, germander or hyssop in Elizabethan gardens (and later, in Jacobean times, in box) were favourite garden features, and designs for them appeared in the new books then being written for gardeners. The scale and number of the knots could be modified to suit the size of the garden, and they were often laid out in small intimate enclosures bounded by hedges, covered walks or raised banks, so that the evergreen patterns could be appreciated close by from a convenient seat, from a raised terrace, or from the windows of the house. According to your pocket and energy you could choose a single knot or a four-square design with a different pattern in each 'quarter', possibly including a maze, or interlaced initials, or a coat of arms. The more complex and fanciful the designs, the more they were admired, and the intricate patterning of the ground, as rich in texture as the silver-gilt interlacing braid stitch on fashionable dress, was pleasing because it was in such contrast to the naturalness of the meadows outside the wall or hedge which enclosed the garden.

Then, as now, it was essential to get the proportions of the design right and to keep the dwarf evergreen hedges well trimmed. 'You should keep your level to a hair, if you fail in this you fail in your whole work', wrote Gervase Markham in the *English Husbandman* of 1613, and he suggested lavender, rosemary, germander, thyme and box as having suitably different tones of green to emphasize the overs and unders of the design. In Pam Watts's 'Knot Garden' on page 70 the hedges would surely have met with his approval, for the Ghiordes knot in which they are worked is perfectly trimmed to a neat upright band calling to mind the 'Little

low Hedges round, like Welts' in Lord Bacon's essay *On Gardens* (1625). The pattern was clearest if the spaces within the knot were filled with coloured materials – brick dust, coal dust, powdered shells and so on – but often they were filled with low-growing flowers 'as pennyroyal, marjoram, camomile, daisies, violets, basil, rue, to give grace to little squares'. In spring and summer the knots were colourful with the flowers enhanced by the green framework, but with well-trimmed hedges the knots were pleasing the whole year 'for these do last all the winter through greene' as Thomas Hill noted in the *Profitable Art of Gardening* (1568).

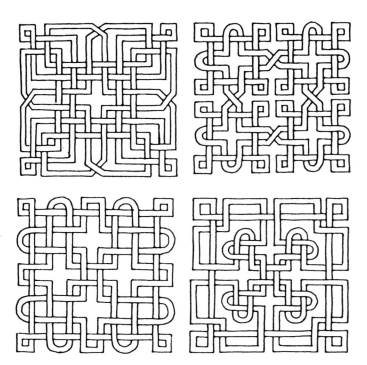

'Proper Knots to be set with Isope and Tyme' from *The Gardener's Labyrinth* of 1577. The top right pattern was probably used for the upper knot in the garden nearest to the High Street at All Souls College opposite. The patterns are ideal for corded quilting.

Woodcuts from Colonna's *Hypnerotomachia* (1499) for clipped box knots.

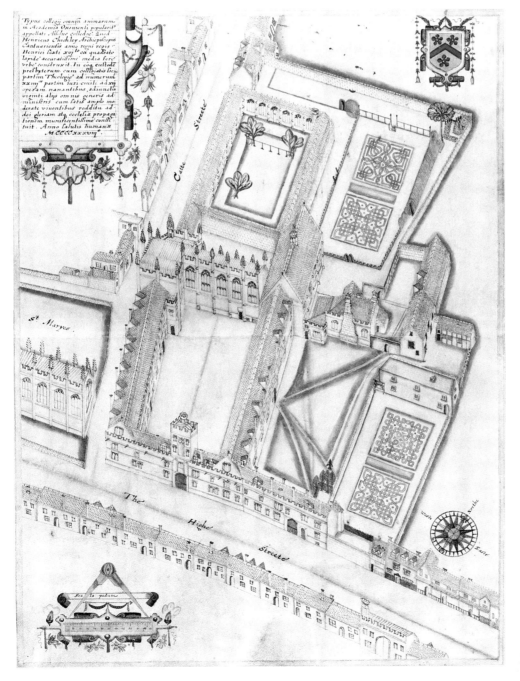

Hovenden's map of All Souls College, Oxford (c1585) shows four complex knot designs in the garden.

'Knot Garden' by Pam Watts. The octagonal garden worked in a variety of canvas stitches including rice, looped half cross, hounds tooth cross and web is exceptionally rich in texture. Matt and glossy threads in many shades of green, pink coral, mauve and violet are combined to render the effect of changing light on flowers and foliage. The dwarf hedges are in Ghiordes knot, using as many as twelve thin strands in the needle at once to create variety of tone, and then clipping the threads to produce a neat upright band. In the centre a woven wheel represents a pool set in gravel of French knots, with four pots of flowers made by working Ghiordes knot over woven wheels.

This aspect of the knots is surely one of the reasons for their return to favour in our gardens. Pleasing to look at most of the year, and appropriate for the smaller gardens of today, they are also soothingly old-fashioned, taking us back to the secluded pleasances of Tudor England remote from the pressures of twentieth-century life. This soothing quality is part of their appeal in needlework too, and they are peculiarly satisfying to stitch on canvas. You need to choose an angular rather than a curved design, and you will find it helpful first to work out, and if necessary simplify, the pattern on graph paper, just as you would when making a real garden knot. In both arts knots are as satisfying to design as to make, time-consuming certainly but in interest and enjoyment well worth the time spent.

The everchanging greens of the living knots transpose well in tufting stitches (see page 93). You could choose silky threads for shiny-leaved box and matt wools for lavender or germander, filling the spaces with a plain stitch like tent and enclosing the garden with a border of mosaic or Scottish stitches. If you decide to fill the knot with flowers, you need to think out the colours and stitches for the whole design rather than filling them in piecemeal. In a restricted colour scheme – pink, grey and mauve; 'sunset' colours; or yellow, white and cream – you could introduce a variety of canvas stitches: web, rice, ray, rococo, diamond eyelets and crossed stitches such as sheaf. If, however, you decide on a wide range of colours, fewer stitches or even a single stitch will unify the design without losing the richness

and profusion – the keynotes of the modern knot garden.

Happily many of the most successful modern creations can be seen in gardens which are open to the public, and they can be an inspiration, no less, to the embroiderer. A visit to the Tudor Garden at Southampton is particularly rewarding. Laid out after the most painstaking research, during which the study of knot gardens in Elizabethan furnishings provided much useful evidence, the knot, taken from *La Maison Rustique* of 1583, is the central feature with the interlace set out in twining threads of winter savory and germander round a diamond of box framed with a wide border of grey-green cotton lavender.

The same pattern can also be seen at Barnsley House in Gloucestershire planted in plain and variegated box interwoven with germander, with a neat dome of *Phillyrea angustifolia* in the centre and two shades of gravel in the spaces. The diverse shades of green change with the light and shadows, and as sunshine catches the young growth along the upper surface of each 'thread' it appears lighter than the sides, with the result that all the threads appear to be double – an effect which you might transpose in couching or two rows of heavy chain. In the Knot Garden at Hatfield House in Hertfordshire, recently laid out in front of the Old Palace, there is a maze and three knots filled with a ravishing mixture of old roses, bulbs and herbaceous plants arranged with unerring skill so that their colours and textures complement one another in a visual feast. The corners of the plots are marked by cones of box for vertical

'Knot Garden' by Susan Smith. Canvas stitches on linen, the design based on one of the knots in *The Gardener's Labyrinth* of 1577.

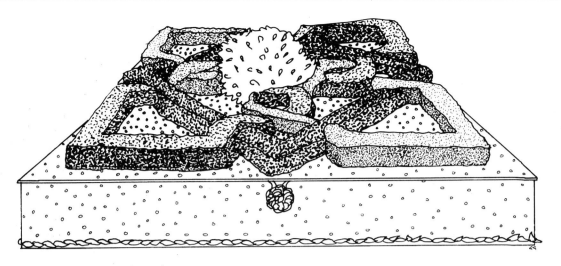

A box design, based on the knot
at Barnsley House, which could
be worked in Ghiordes knot on
a tent-stitch ground.

interest and there are tiered 'cake stands' of holly whose eye-catching shapes may determine you to try a perspective rather than an aerial view, using the mellow tones of brick in the Old Palace as your background. The knots and maze can be viewed from above, as they lie below grassy slopes planted with bulbs and wild flowers and cut only once a year. This is another possible subject for embroidery, treating the 'flowery mead' effect of the slopes as a wide border of free stitchery enclosing the regular patterning of the knots.

Do consider how you will use your knot before you begin. When looking at finished work, I am often struck by the different effects of light on an embroidered surface, depending on whether it is placed upright or set horizontally. It seems to me that this is something that should be taken into much greater consideration before automatically framing a piece and hanging it upright on the wall, so exposing it to more or less direct illumination. Light falling obliquely on a rich embroidered surface lying flat or at a slight angle can create magical effects, comparable to the subtlety of early morning or evening light in the garden, as opposed to the flat brightness of the direct midday sunshine. This is a reason for choosing knot patterns for cushions, bedspreads and rugs which are meant to be seen from above. They also look well set into table tops covered with glass for protection, and small boxes, pincushions or book covers add interest to any tablescape.

The old knot designs in this chapter can easily be enlarged to the size you need by photocopy and can be stitched in a great variety of methods. Some of the so-called 'plaine knots' are far too complex to set out in the garden but their linear quality makes them ideal for machine embroidery. An easy way to transfer the design is to place stiff transparent muslin over the photocopy and trace the outline onto it in pencil. Put the muslin over your chosen material and stretch both layers in a frame with the muslin uppermost; you can then follow the most complex interlace accurately with the needle, having removed the foot and covered the feed. If perlé or other thick thread is wound in the bobbin (cable stitch) with the top tension tight and the lower tension loose, a slightly raised and bobbly line will effectively recreate the garden knot. Green would be an obvious choice, or you could follow Markham's directions for a knot planted in 'several threads of one kinde and colour, as thus for example; in one thread plant your carnation gillyflower, in another your great white gillyflower, in another your mingled gillyflower, and in another your blood red gillyflower'.

(*opposite*) Plan of the Tudor
Garden at Southampton, with
the knot in the centre. The
garden was designed by Sylvia
Landsberg and features include
a fountain plot, arbour,
covered walk and bee skeps in
a tiny 'secret' garden (plan
drawn by Alan Williams).

(*opposite*) The knot from *La
Maison Rustique* (1583) used
as a pattern in the Tudor
garden and for the Barnsley
box design above.

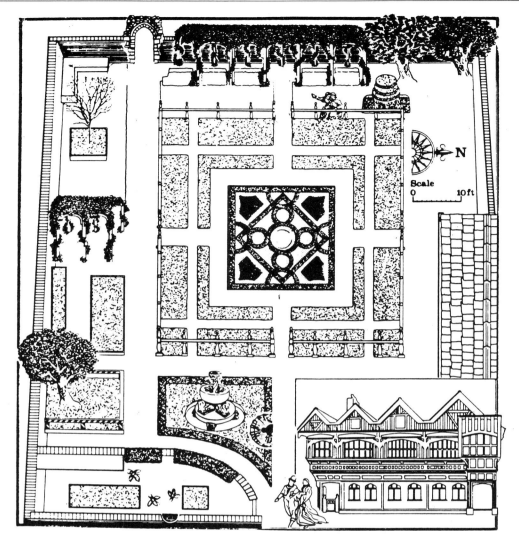

Knot from *Embroidery* (1909).

A twentieth-century knot design from Edward Kemp's *How to Lay Out a Garden*, which could be used for inlay or quilting.

'Elizabethan Garden' by Audrey Ormrod worked in cross stitch in stranded cottons on linen, the colours chosen to represent the diversity of flowers in the beds. The garden is depicted as a flat plan with the house in elevation.

opposite Rug embroidered by Helen Williams whose work as an illustrator often includes minutely detailed knot and interlace patterns. Here she enjoys working on a larger scale in thick wools on rug canvas.

'Proper knots to be cast in the four quarters of a garden' from *The Gardener's Labyrinth* of 1577, and perfect for a set of cushions in appliqué.

Tulips and hyacinths were another possibility, so that 'it shall appear like a knot of diverse coloured ribbons, most pleasing and most rare'. For this you might choose reds and pinks, possibly winding two different shades on the spool for the 'mingled' effect, or you could experiment with the narrow ribbons now available. A small box I made in natural Thai silk had a knot embroidered in cable stitch on the lid, the pattern taken from *The Compleat Gardener's Practice* of 1664 by Stephen Blake. In his book each design is accompanied by a verse couplet (see page 81), and so I embroidered this round the sides of the box; an interlace border would have been equally suitable.

Blake suggests that you could 'modelize and contrive your garden plots' with 'knots of my invention or those that may be invented by yourself which probably please your fancy better than mine'. If you do decide to make up your own knots, you might try following an exercise suggested in *Embroidery* (a volume of articles edited by Grace Christie and published by Pearsall in 1909). First you make a continuous band, second you indent the sides, third you twist the points of the indented sides into loops. Then you draw out the same figures again and add a second band, treating it in the same manner. Further elaboration – floral sprigs in the spaces and tiny patterns worked within the bands – could easily be worked out, provided care was taken with the overs and unders of the bands, as I found myself when I worked a set of cushions to this design on parchment-coloured glazed chintz with the bands in two shades of gold and cornflowers in the spaces. I machined the knot, but I was tempted to lay it in braid couched with blue to match the flowers and the thick piping that edged the cushions. Indeed the charm of knots is that they are endlessly adaptable and can be just as effective whether you choose the simplest or the most demanding methods.

Knot with a continuous band border from *The Gardener's Labyrinth*.

Four different patterns fill the 'quarters' in this plan from *A Short Instruction* of 1592. They could be worked in corded quilting with the decorative border of tiny trees in tied quilting.

Knot designs from *The Country House-wife's Garden* by William Lawson (1617).

'Elizabethan Garden' by Kate Wells. Hand and machine embroidery combined on a painted calico ground. The flowers are hand stitched in French knots, satin stitch, seeding and needlepunch. The trees are machined on an industrial Irish machine, and the grass of the 'quarters' is ingeniously rendered by rows of machine whip stitch with the top thread removed to create blades of grass.

Maze pattern from *Le Jardin de Plaisir* by André Mollet (1628).

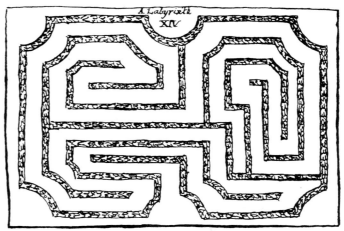

Labyrinth from *The Solitary or Carthusian Gardener* (1706).

'Maze of the Four Seasons' by Kate Wells. Hand and machine embroidery on Colourfun painted calico. Hedges tufted using the 'tailor tacking' foot on a Bernina machine, wallflower borders tufted with needlepunch and the landscape views of the North Yorkshire dales outline embroidered on an industrial Irish machine with hand embroidery in split and satin stitch.

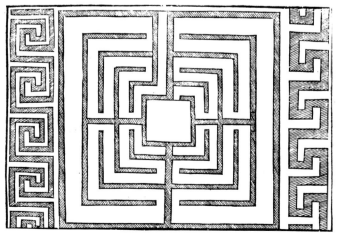

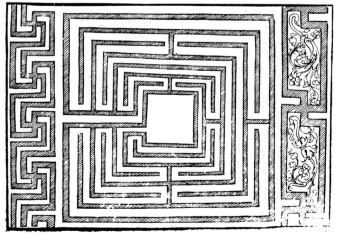

Two designs by Serlio for mazes (1566).

'In this knot the crossing bands which divide the surface up into panels interweave, each going alternatively over and under those which it encounters.' The design comes from an article on knot designs by A. H. Christie, Grace Christie's husband, in *Embroidery* (1909).

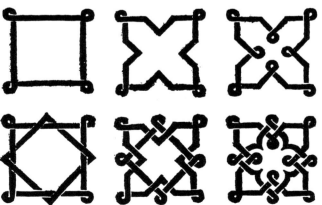

An exercise in knot making from *Embroidery* (1909).

Knots from *The Compleat Gardener's Practice* by Stephen Blake (1664).

Here have I made the true Lover's Knott
To try it in Mariage was never my Lot

Cross diamonds in the paper I doe frame
And in the ground I can draw the same

6

TOPIARY

In making knots the imagination is to some extent controlled by the patterns, but in topiary – the art of clipping evergreens into ornamental shapes varying in complexity from balls, cones and pyramids to birds, animals, what you will – the only limit to creating the most elaborate fantasies is the willingness of the shrubs to retain the shapes imposed on them, and the patience to trim them up over many seasons. In embroidery, what attracts us, as well as the fanciful appeal, are the exciting possibilities of texture and shape, and here the only limit lies in finding an appropriate method and materials to interpret our ideas. Canvaswork, contemporary stumpwork, machine embroidery, appliqué, patchwork and quilting all have their merits and can be tried out alone or variously combined. You can work in the finest materials on a tiny scale as in Susan Smith's 'Clipped Yew' (below), or devise means of making a complete three-dimensional 'garden room' with eccentric peacocks and walls of yew seven foot long and over four feet wide as in Mary Cozens-Walker's 'Topiary Garden' (opposite).

Topiary was invented by the Romans who indulged in flights of fancy that seem extraordinary even today. Hedges of cypress trimmed into walls, their tops ornamented with hunting scenes and fleets of ships were known to Pliny, and his nephew, Pliny the Younger, described his own garden in Tuscany which had a double row of box trees cut in the shapes of animals and evergreen hedges 'cut in a variety of forms'. Box was also set out and trimmed into the name of the owner and his gardener, and used to form compartments and small obelisks.

Pliny's description was eagerly taken up by Renaissance enthusiasts, as keen to interpret the culture of Greece and Rome in their gardens as in all the arts. The great pleasure gardens of Italy were divided into compartments separated by clipped hedges, some of them boasting amazing collections of topiary figures including dragons, centaurs, owls, wild boar, dolphins, philosophers 'and more things of a like kind'. The fashion spread all over Europe in the sixteenth century. In 1599 the Swiss traveller Thomas Platter visited Whitehall where he saw 'all manner of shapes, men and women, half men and half horses, sirens, serving maids with baskets, French lilies, and delicate crenellations all round'. We can appreciate the effect of such creations today at Levens Hall in Cumbria, where there is a unique survival of a late Renaissance topiary garden set out in the 1690s with trees and bushes cut out in the most curious shapes. It is a spellbinding place, especially in the evening when the shapes cast unexpected shadows and the figures seem to take on a life of their own.

With its long tradition for naïve and fanciful representation, embroidery is a perfect medium for topiary. It can conjure up the seemingly magical atmosphere of the topiary garden and take us back to the wonder of childhood

'Clipped Yew' by Susan Smith. Counted and drawn thread on lemon coloured linen 29 to 1in (840 stitches to the sq in). The design is worked out on graph paper, and the difficulty of rendering curves on evenweave is overcome by using tent stitch on a tiny scale. The panel is part of a 'topiary suite' which includes diminutive holm oaks and mop-headed box.

opposite 'The Topiary Garden' and 'The Headboard' by Mary Cozens-Walker were both inspired by seventeenth-century formal gardens. In 'The

Topiary Garden' the lawn is towelling dyed two shades of green, painted and stretched, and the hedges and topiary birds are made with a wooden base, chicken wire and tailored calico. Wood shavings and sawdust were applied to this and the entire surface was painted. The irresistible idea of sitting up in bed supported by a headboard made of topiary shapes as if in a garden was realized in practical terms by looping and tufting in wool and cotton with machine wrapped twigs and some hand stitchery to simulate the texture of yew foliage. The lawn between the shapes was made from velvet, quilted and spray painted to indicate shadows. Padded velvet was also used for the distant shapes against the background trellis.

This illustration of topiary shapes by John Farleigh from *Old Fashioned Flowers* by Sacheverell Sitwell (1939) would transpose perfectly in speckling stitches.

A topiary enclosure that might 'come out of a book of fairy tales to enchant the eyes of childhood' from Viscountess Wolseley's *Gardens: Their Form and Design* (1919).

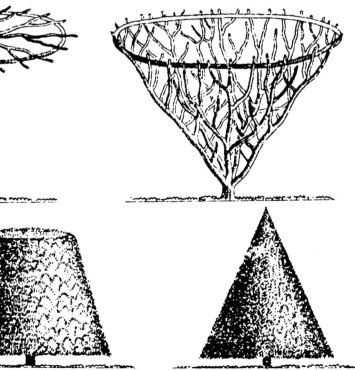

Various topiary shapes from M. Boitard's *l'Architecte des Jardins* (1845).

'Topiary Birds' by Janet Haigh. Canvaswork picture using stranded cottons pulled apart and reblended with four different shades in the needle mainly in encroaching and diagonal stitches.

'Topiary Allotment' by Belinda Downes inspired by the topiary at Hidcote in Gloucestershire. Contemporary stumpwork on a painted and shadow quilted ground with the fence in needleweaving.

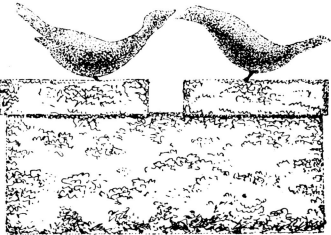

'Birds on a Hedge' from *Gardens: Their Form and Design.*

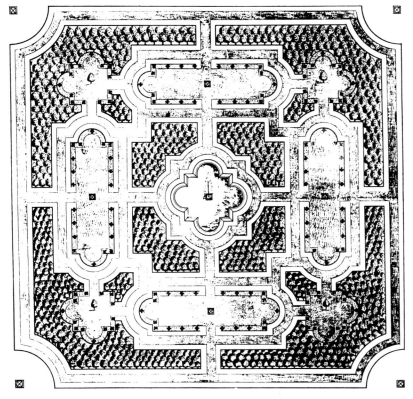

Parterre patterns from André Mollet's *Le Jardin de Plaisir* (1628).

A parterre of embroidery from Pluche's *Spectacle de la Nature* (1740) which closely resembles a waistcoat design for quilting or appliqué.

Parterres of embroidery and a curious clock sundial reminiscent of patchwork from J. C. Volkamer's *Nürnbergische Hesperides* (1708–14). The plates depict citrus fruit collected by the author and his friends, and vignettes of their gardens in and around Nürnberg.

imaginings. The birds on Janet Haigh's hedge on page 86 are examples of topiary in its most fanciful guise – one of them has actually taken to the air – used as in the real garden as free-standing shapes set out singly, or in groups or rows, or ornamenting the top of a hedge. But she also illustrates topiary's more common use as a kind of green architecture, essential in laying out formal gardens both past and present. Its heyday was in the seventeenth and early eighteenth centuries when box, yew, holly and phillyrea were the principal plants trimmed into cones, spheres and spirals to emphasize the symmetry and unity of the designs. Hornbeam was clipped into great avenues, and box was used in the elaborate scrollwork of the *parterres de broderie*.

The word 'parterre' means 'along the ground', and it describes the free-flowing patterns which made the intricacies of the earlier knots, each with its own pattern, look old-fashioned. In 1664 John Evelyn saw a splendid parterre in the Luxembourg Gardens, and noted that it was 'so rarely designed and so accurately kept that the embroidery makes a stupendious effect to the lodgings in front of it'. Extending like a great carpet in front of the main façade of the house and closely related to its design, the parterre was best seen from the central window of the first floor, or failing that from a raised terrace; any other viewpoint would distort the patterns. Most parterre designs were rectangular in their overall plan, extending away from the house with symmetrical patterns set out in pairs on either side of a broad allée, and they were generally on a far larger scale than the knots. Their overall symmetry, with the halves or quarters of the parterre to left and right of a central axis, was notably like the balanced embroidery patterns on contemporary dress. Some of the designs exactly resemble waistcoat patterns drawn out ready for working and can be adapted for this purpose today. The exuberant flowing lines work particularly well in crewel work and quilting, or they could be couched in thick twisted yarn or cord. Designs for single rectangular parterres might be used for book covers, and quartered ones for cushions or box tops.

Both knots and parterres are really forms of topiary; they are essentially artificial, and it was inevitable that they should be swept away together with the straight, clipped allées when the vogue for landscaping and 'naturalness' came in in the eighteenth century. But not for long; as soon as formality began to reappear in nineteenth-century gardens, topiary was there too, making an Egyptian pyramid at Biddulph Grange in Staffordshire, a sundial at Ascott, Buckinghamshire and playing cards at Ludstone Hall in Shropshire. Shirley Hibberd writing in the 1870s summed up its appeal: 'It may be true, as I believe it is, that the natural form of a tree is the most beautiful possible, but it may happen that we do not always want the most beautiful form, but one of our own designing, and expressive of our ingenuity.'

This surely is why topiary still flourishes in all its shapes and forms, from the breath-taking restoration of the great parterres at Het Loo in Holland, to the single guardian peacock in the cottage garden. It thrives, because it is not only intriguing to look at but such fun to do. In my garden I endeavour to shape my peacock and cones of box as carefully as a proper topiarist should, so that they stand out well from other plants. In embroidery I try to find equivalents in stitches and thread – fine silks and synthetic yarns in machine satin and whip stitch worked in spirals, thicker threads wound on the bobbin and worked from the reverse. I experiment with threads shaded from light to dark and back again to see if these will capture the effects of light and shade which are part of the charm of topiary: 'In sunshine it glistens in countless facets of reflected light, while in shadow its sombre darkness is almost black. Topiary is equally effective standing against bright green turf, or silhouetted clear cut against blue sky', wrote Percy Cane in *Garden Design of Today* (1934).

Whatever form your needlework takes, do study the clipped surface of the plants used in topiary in the real garden, as their varying textures will suggest different stitches and methods to you.

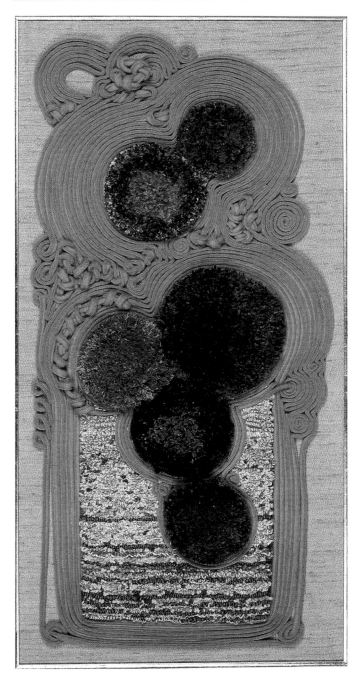

'Parterre' by Erika Korzim inspired by memories of baroque gardens in her native Hungary and worked on a large scale in handwoven and corded wools.

opposite 'Stone Green Hall' by Jenny Chippindale. Patchwork hanging in dyed and sprayed calico with some surface stitchery and broderie anglaise in the girl's dress.

'Beppo' by Diana Springall. Low relief panel in wool, felt-covered cord and tufting on a dupion ground.

Raked sand and stone garden from Josiah Conder's *Landscape Gardening in Japan* (1912). Raked-sand patterns transpose well in couching, quilting or machine whip stitch.

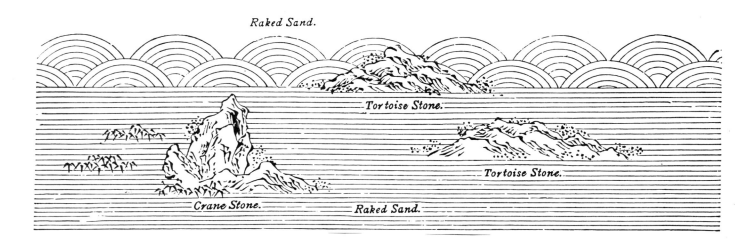

Raked Sand.

Tortoise Stone.

Tortoise Stone.

Crane Stone.

Raked Sand.

Topiary as green architecture in the gardens of Marly near Versailles in 1713.

'A Garden of Limitless View' from *Landscape Gardening in Japan.* Water and trees create an artificial landscape as carefully designed as their counterparts embroidered on kimonos.

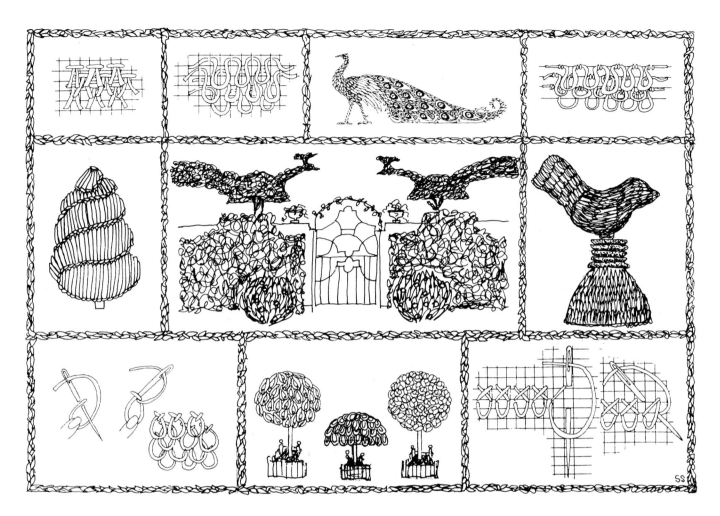

Smooth shaven yew in dark green or gold gives the densest texture and this might be conveyed on evenweave in closely worked diagonal, encroaching or plaited Gobelin stitch. Compare these effects with the technique used in the 'Topiary Gardens, Great Dixter' (see page 31) in which close machining provides textural interest and trapunto quilting brings out the forms. Box in plain green, or variegated in silver or gold, has a lighter looser texture, holly is glossy, cypress matt and feathery. These qualities can be combined and contrasted to make striking garden pictures – box balls and pyramids backed by yew hedges, dark columns of holly against walls of soft blue cypress which may tempt you to transpose the shapes in appliqué or the texture in free stitchery, or to use tufting to convey both texture and form together. If you combine matt and shiny threads, tufting can echo the changing light on foliage and produce the subtlest effects. In machine embroidery it can be worked using the looping foot or rug fork on the Elna machine or the tailor's tacking foot on the Bernina, and by hand you can choose between Ghiordes knot, Surrey or velvet stitch.

In a series of low relief panels inspired by the Japanese gardens in Kyoto (page 90), Diana Springall combines stranded and perlé cotton to suggest the bright vibrant leaves of flowering azaleas clipped into balls. This use of topiary may seem strange to Western eyes, but in both the real gardens and in the embroidery, the verdant balls find a perfect foil in the matt surface of raked sand, rendered in these panels in felt cord on a dupion ground. The panels, so satisfying in their abstract shapes and patterning, invite quiet

Stitches for topiary, (*top row from left to right*) Ghiordes knot (single knot tufting), looped running and looped couching; (*middle row*) topiary cone in closely worked buttonhole stitch, the birds in the centre, based on a drawing by Edwin Lutyens in free machine embroidery, and the bird on the right in rows of chain stitch; (*bottom row*) detached loop stitch and velvet stitch with the box trees in detached chain stitch and French knots.

contemplation, just as their real counterparts do in Japanese gardens where rocks, water, sand and plants have a symbolic meaning. The evergreen azaleas, for example, were chosen to represent eternal rather than ephemeral beauty, and the flowers were shorn because they were frivolous.

Anyone who doubts the power of embroidery to express the atmosphere of the garden, as well as to record its patterns, should study this panel and the patchwork hanging on page 91. A mood of dreamy contemplation pervades the garden at Stone Green Hall in Kent depicted here. The shapes and varied tones of the individual leaves of the pleached hornbeams are suggested in the triangles of patchwork, and the harmonies of green in the grass and the great domes of box add to the serenity of the scene. The uncanny power of topiary to people the garden is wonderfully conveyed here; a solitary figure sits on the lawn, alone – but not alone; the topiary surrounds her with its friendly presence.

7

USING THE HERBALS

One of the richest sources for garden embroidery is to be found in the printed herbals and flower books which began to appear at the end of the fifteenth century and whose heyday was in the sixteenth and early seventeenth centuries. These beautiful volumes can be consulted in specialist libraries, but for practical purposes it is more convenient to make use of readily available books. One of the most useful is the *Handbook of Plant and Floral Ornament* (first published in 1909 as the *Craftsman's Plant Book*) in which Ralph Hatton gathered together over a thousand illustrations suitable for designs. They were, he wrote, 'full of decorative suggestion and fine examples of treatment, they present the plants as they are known to ordinary people, with their character usually admirably expressed . . . in many cases they are designs ready-done and can be appropriated wholesale'.

In her embroidered book, 'English Gardens', Julia Barton has 'appropriated' and slightly modified a collection of plants from herbals and flower books, choosing each one to epitomize a stage in the development of gardens in England. Plant and garden are set side by side on each double-page spread, the 'pages' being calico overlaid with painted silk organza. Thus the bramble from the Bury St Edmunds *Herbal of Apuleius* dated 1120 faces the medieval plot in which it grew, and the pink from Clusius' work of 1583 faces an Elizabethan knot garden typical of the period. The book is bound within green-velvet covers and is as delightful to handle as the volumes which inspired it. A herbal described

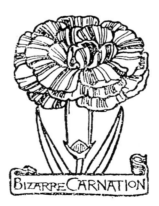

Carnation design (above left) from *Gardens: Their Form and Design*, possibly based on great gillyflowers (below left) from the *Hortus Floridus* of Crispin de Pass (1615).

Carnations and pinks were favourites in both gardens and embroidery at the time. The bizarre carnation and picotee are taken from *The Craftsman's Plant Book* by Ralph Hatton.

Julia Barton's book, 'English Gardens', open at the Elizabethan knot-garden spread. A machine-embroidered pink faces the garden where the knot pattern is couched in thick wool filled with flowers in French knots. The border and ground are stencilled and sprayed to repeat the knot designs.

Dianthus from de l'Écluse's herbal of 1583 adapted and worked by Julia Barton in her book.

'English Gardens' by Julia Barton, an embroidered book of great originality and charm bound in green velvet with the title letters applied in red leather. The 'end papers' of marbled silk can just be seen.

Strawberry, *Fragaria vesca*, from Fuchs's herbal of 1542. The clear outline of the woodcut makes the plant easy to adapt for a design whereas the strawberry (top right) from Gerard's *Herbal* of 1597 would need to be much simplified to be effective. The small strawberry motifs are from *A Scholehouse for the Needle* by Richard Shorleyker (1632).

plants which were thought to be useful, and a flower book or florilegium was more concerned with plants grown for their beauty.

What satisfaction these books must have given to their first owners as they studied the illustrations to identify their new acquisitions and learn about their uses and cultivation. The early botanical artists tried to explain the essential character of the plants in outline. Otto Brunfels called his lovely herbal printed in 1530 *Living Portraits of Plants* and great care was taken to convey the structure and details of growth in the drawing of the plant on the woodblock, which was the first stage in making the woodcuts which illustrated such early printed herbals. The next stage was to cut away the background leaving only the outline to come in contact with the ink roller. The results were bold and clear and, far from being a limitation, the rectangular shape of the woodblock resulted in the plant being presented in a strikingly decorative manner.

William Morris collected sixteenth-century herbals and read their text for advice on the properties of dye plants. At the same time he undoubtedly saw the value of the woodcuts for designs. He studied every detail of the plants in his own garden and would have appreciated the clear way the woodcuts displayed each plant's character. He had a unique gift for transforming the plants he loved into lively designs, many of them reminiscent of garden pleasures, and the herbals were among the sources of inspiration he had in mind when in 1899 he gave a lecture on Pattern Designing. He said:

> However original a man may be, he cannot afford to disregard the works of art that have been produced in times past when design was flourishing; he's bound to study the old examples and get what is good out of them without making a design which lays itself open to plagiarism. No doubt the only help out of that is for a man to be always drawing from nature getting the habit of knowing what beautiful forms and lines are; that I think is a positive necessity.

If you take Morris's advice and 'get what is good' out of the herbals you will in the process learn a great deal about good design, especially if you study the living plant and the woodcut illustration together and try to analyse how the artist simplified and spread it out to fill the shape of the block. As an experiment, go into your garden and choose a plant or sprig to match one of the woodcuts in this chapter. Hold it in your hand, as this invites the closest examination, and then set it on a sheet of paper in front of you. Try to make a simple outline sketch of it and then, and only then, compare your version with the woodcut. You will probably find that you have not simplified your subject sufficiently to make a working design, but if you persevere you will soon learn how to eliminate unnecessary detail and make the plant fill the space you want. If you do not feel confident enough to sketch the plants from life, or copy the woodcuts freehand, take Ralph Hatton's advice and trace them: 'If the reader will follow the lines, he will find how free and swift they are.' Tracing paper is also invaluable if you want to adapt an illustration. Many of the herbals depict the plant with its bulb or root, which can be decorative, but may not be what you want to include. There may be too many stems, flowerheads, buds or leaves, or the plant may fill a rectangular space when you need a design for a square one. The best way of altering the plant, without losing the essential character which attracted you in the first place, is to trace the main stems and leaves lightly in pencil and then, when you feel you are nearing an outline you can use, go over it in black felt-tip pen.

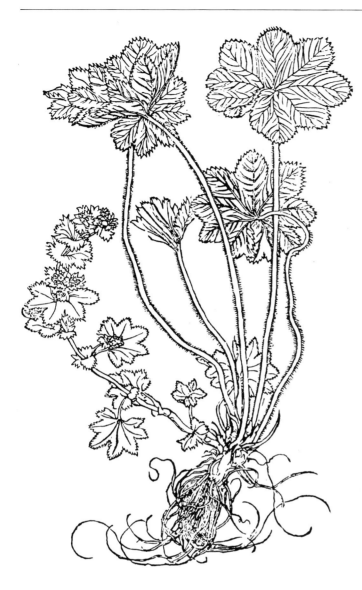

Alchemilla vulgaris, one of Brunfel's 'plant portraits', depicted with its roots whose undulating lines could be decoratively treated in a design.

Title page from the *Grete Herbal* (1526) with mandrake figures and formalized plants and trees.

VERONICA · FOXGLOVE · LADY'S SLIPPER · BRASSIA · WILLOW-HERB

CROCUS · SELF-HEAL · TRUE-LOVE · GLADIOLUS · BORAGE

'Jacobean Wood'; a cushion designed for the National Trust by Kaffe Fassett inspired by engravings of seventeenth-century flowers in the author's *Embroidered Gardens* (1979).

Flower designs by Ralph Hatton, from his *Handbook*.

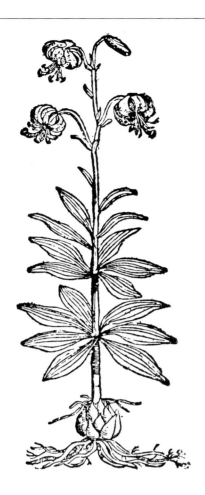

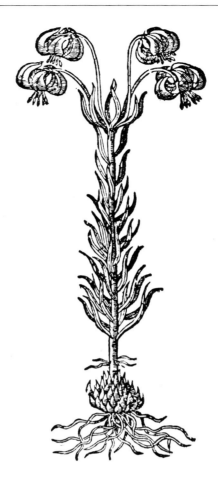

Boldly defined turk's cap and red martagon lilies from de Lobel's herbal of 1581 similar in style to Julia Barton's lily below.

The formal garden spread from Julia Barton's book with a martagon or turk's head lily from a Venetian herbal facing a parterre of embroidery.

Diagram by Walter Crane showing how to design a repeating pattern of tulips and daisies.

I am convinced that the more you familiarize yourself with good designs, adapting them to suit your purpose where necessary, the more likely you are to take the next step and begin drawing and designing yourself. Indeed the fact that you have chosen a particular motif means that you have already made the first step towards designing. Try using the same motif in a number of different arrangements. Set side by side you will have a simple border which can be varied by altering the size. You could repeat the motif all over the ground at even intervals or in groups, or you could set them within a framework as described in the chapter on knots. Discussing the use of plants as an element in design Ralph Hatton wrote: 'Designing comes down ultimately to space filling, for unless the spaces are properly filled they lose their shape and are not what they are supposed to be. Indeed good space filling preserves good spacing, and without it good spacing is of no avail.'

Simple sprigs and groups of dots in a well-balanced design from May Morris's *Decorative Needlework* (1893).

A repeating design of slips of flowers based on a Jacobean bodice from Grace Christie's *Embroidery and Tapestry Weaving* (1906).

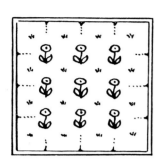

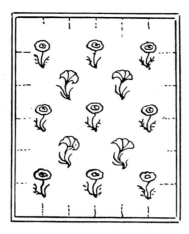

Arrangement of flower slips in 'powdering' from Joan Drew's *Embroidery and Design.*

The herbal artists who most interest the embroiderer are those who draw the plants boldly in outline with the minimum of shading. The strawberry from Leonhard Fuchs's *De Historia Stirpium* (1542) is a fine example 'positively delineated according to the features and likeness of living plants', with none of the 'shadows' used by some artists. The illustrations in this and many other contemporary books were intended to be coloured by their owners. Crispin de Pass in his *Hortus Floridus* (1615) even gives detailed instructions concerning colours like 'mayden's blush' and 'verdigreece', and painting was considered a way of becoming better acquainted with the plants and making the record more personal. The tiny creatures – insects, butterflies, even a small mouse – which enliven the pages, and the plants, are depicted from a low viewpoint, almost as if from a mouse's-eye view.

Mouse's-eye view of the saffron crocus from the *Hortus Floridus* of Crispin de Pass.

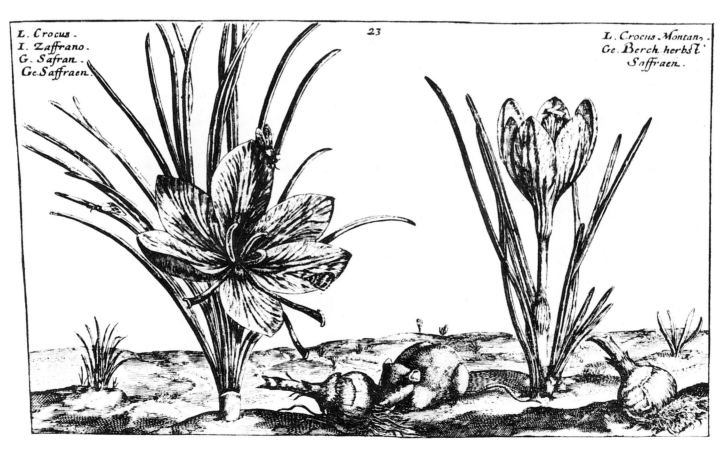

Anemones from *Le Jardin d'Hyver.*

The book is divided into sections to illustrate the flowers of the four seasons, and it reflects the passionate interest of the age in collecting the widest possible range of plants. The wonderfully decorative plates in Besler's *Hortus Eystettensis* (1613) are also arranged by seasons, and record the actual plants in the gardens of the Bishop of Eistatt in Bavaria; while Franeau's *Le Jardin d'Hyver* (1616) was so called because it was intended as a substitute garden for enjoyment in winter. These surely are ideas to develop in embroidery – the making of your own 'flower garden' or 'Hortus Floridus', recording the plants which gave you particular pleasure during the year. To turn the pages of a finely illustrated book, like the slow unwinding of a beautiful Japanese scroll, is a different pleasure from looking at a picture on a wall. True, it is visual, but it is more intimate – a leisurely process which you can share with, perhaps, one other person or enjoy on your own. To show such a book to a fellow enthusiast would be a double pleasure, as the embroidery could, if well and imaginatively done, reveal new and unsuspected qualities in the chosen plants.

Your embroidered herbal or florilegium could illustrate a single season's plants, or a particular family of flowers – one charming seventeenth-century work was devoted entirely to anemones – or it could bring together plants whose textures and forms you have studied in detail. The pages (like those in Julia Barton's book) could be soft as in a child's rag book, or made of stiff card with the embroidery mounted separately. Whichever you choose you will have to devise a binding to hold together and protect your work. Exquisite embroidered bindings using canvaswork, metal threads or stumpwork were made in the Elizabethan and Stuart periods, yet they are rarely seen today. This is a pity, as a book lying on a table shows the textural quality of the stitchery to particularly good advantage. Your cover might depict the garden where the flowers were grown or, as it is a personal record, you might prefer to use decorative lettering with the title and your name or initials combined in the design. If you wanted to present the flowers with a verse or description, as was often the case in the early books, you might consider using transfer paints or crayons with Letraset, or write freehand in machine embroidery.

Hyacinths and ornithogalum from Besler's *Hortus Eystettensis.*

Houseleek from Colonna's *Ekphrasis* set off by a border of printer's 'flowers'.

A basket of roses, pinks and other flowers from the title page of *The Craftsman's Plant Book.*

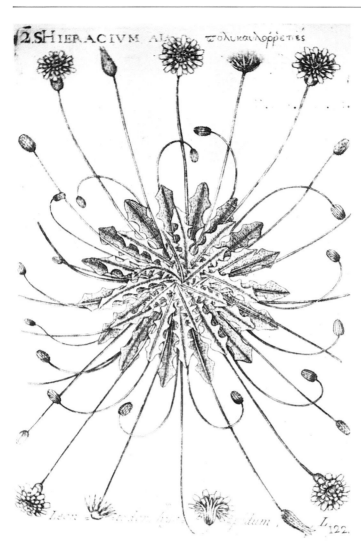

Hawkweed seen from above, by de Belleval, forming a beautiful, balanced pattern.

Some of the herbals presented the plants within a decorative border, and this is another treatment worth considering for either the cover or the pages or both. Fabio Colonna's *Ekphrasis . . . Stirpium* or *Description of Plants* (1616) was one of the earliest works illustrated with pure etching which gives a more delicate line than woodcuts. The plants, like the houseleek with its extraordinary geometric forms – triangles, pentagons and hexagons – so suggestive of stitchery, are framed in heavy borders of printer's 'flowers' reminiscent of blackwork and which provide a neat crisp finish. Particularly apt for needlework designs are the plant drawings engraved for Pierre Richer de Belleval at the end of the sixteenth century but not published until 1796. De Belleval was the founder of the famous botanic garden at Montpellier in southern France and it was here that J. E. Gilibert found and bought the engravings to illustrate his *Démonstrations Élémentaires de la Botanique*. Look at the marvellous radial design of the hawkweed or the formalized flowers of the alpine clematis; de Belleval's unique style emphasizes the character of the plants, striking a rare balance between naturalness and formality. His illustrations, like those of so many of these botanical artists, are an inspiration and delight to use.

Alpine clematis by de Belleval seen in cross section.

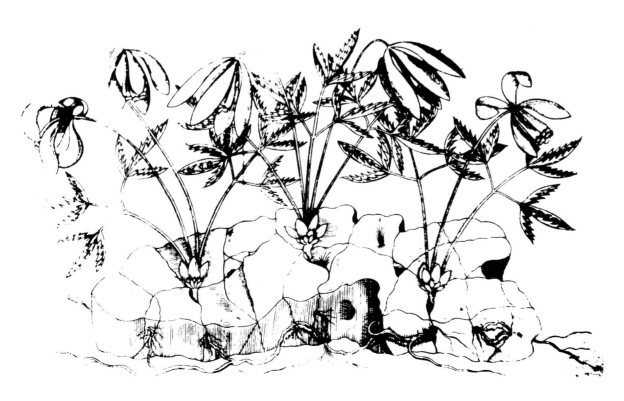

8

FLOWERS AND FOLIAGE

'The successful gardener does not use all the plants that exist, but experience has taught him or her to select and put together the right plants – right in texture, scale and colour and this is a necessary part of the best embroidery.'

Louisa Pesel

For many people a garden means first and foremost a place to grow flowers. Long vistas of grass, water and trees are admirable in landscape gardens but at home, where space is restricted, variety and interest is provided by flowers. Yet far too often our small modern gardens are dull, both in the choice of flowers and the way they are planted. It is ironic that as gardens get smaller the choice of flowers gets larger, and this makes selecting and putting together the right plants all the more difficult. Not nearly enough attention is paid to thinking out the planting as a design, and here I am convinced that the concerns of embroidery really can benefit the garden and vice versa.

In the real garden the flowers (and in this chapter I include shrubs, trees and plants with ornamental leaves) are grouped formally and informally in many different ways – in beds and borders of regular and irregular shapes, in rock and wall gardens, and in grass as in flowery meads or meadow gardens. The effect they make will depend on the skill of the gardener or embroiderer in combining them to complement one another in colour, texture and form; this skill can only be acquired by close observation of the plants and an understanding of balance and proportion, which are the cardinal rules of good design. The more you study and analyse imaginative planting schemes when garden visiting, the easier you will find the selection and arrangement of flowers in your embroidered garden.

Let us begin with the flower border. In embroidery, a border means a decorative band or edge round or along a design; in the garden a border surrounds and enhances a lawn, pool or central feature, or runs along one or both sides of a path or walk. Borders vary in width, and the narrowest, or ribbon border, makes a good subject for a simple design. Here the plants are arranged in the manner of a frieze, spaced so that you can appreciate their shape. This arrangement looks well in furnishing embroideries such as curtains and bedspreads, and is especially effective on screens, as can be seen in Sue Rangeley's three-fold screen inspired by hollyhocks. It is surprising that screens are not more often used as a means of displaying and using embroidery. Anyone who has seen the exquisite flowers painted on Japanese screens, often wide enough to be used as room-dividers, will appreciate the subtle way the panels separate yet strengthen the design. A four-fold screen – it could be a miniature one not more than a few inches high – might illustrate the growth of, say, a rose border through the seasons from winter leaflessness to spring growth, summer flowers and autumn hips.

'Hollyhock screen' by Sue Rangeley. Threefold screen machine-quilted in silk, the flowers sprayed in different tones through stencils with some hand painting and stitchery on the flowers and butterflies.

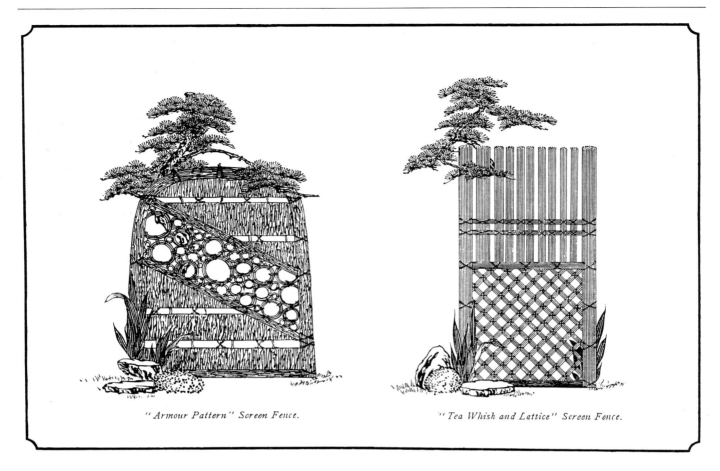

" Armour Pattern" Screen Fence.   *" Tea Whisk and Lattice" Screen Fence.*

Fence patterns from Josiah
Conder's *Landscape Gardening
in Japan* suggest pulled work or
needleweaving.

Ribbon border against a hedge
cut with a rounded top from
*The Art and Craft of Garden
Making* by Thomas Mawson
(1900).

Border designs from Miss
Higgin's *Handbook of
Embroidery* (1912).

In a ribbon border the plants can be seen silhouetted against the background of a hedge or wall. An interesting way to try out plants for a needlework border design is to experiment in the garden on a bright day with flowers you have picked. Remove excess leaves from the lower part of their stems and hold them against a large sheet of white card. Then let the sun cast shadows on the card, and move the flowers gently to see how they look best. Get a friend to photograph the card or, holding a flower in one hand, follow its outline on the card with the other hand using a felt-tip pen. Even better, put a sheet of tracing paper over the white card and draw on this. Then you will have the beginnings of a design which you can simplify and try out against different backgrounds.

Whether your border is narrow or deep, your background should act as a foil to the flowers and should not be too obtrusive or fussy. In a real garden see how the largely dark background of the straight-clipped surface of yew or box hedge provides continuity and how the texture, colour and shapes of border plants stand out against it. The green tones of the hedge are varied nonetheless by the interplay of light and shade, and this you might suggest by stippling on a painted or sprayed ground, or by working differently shaded strands of thread together in the needle in unassertive stitches like tent, gobelin, bricking or plait. Tapestry hedges which combine mixtures of box, yew, holly, copper or plain beech to interweave and create a richly varied surface are fascinating to explore in embroidery. But if you choose this as your ground, take care that it does not swamp the flowers. To keep the balance in your composition try repeating versions of a single flower, groups of delphinium in tones of blue or tall creamy foxgloves, against the diverse tones of the hedge.

Stone and brick walls also provide sympathetic backgrounds to borders, and their regular or random patterns can be worked in canvas, appliqué or quilting. Some borders are planted against fences, and these too make

Fences in needleweaving, laidwork or quilting make interesting backgrounds for borders of flowers.

Baskets of flowers set out on the lawn.

interesting grounds. Look at the strong verticals of posts or stakes set side by side or spaced at regular intervals, and the coarse texture of wattle and larchlap, and see how well these would transpose in pulled work, needleweaving or simple weaving together of strips of torn material, ribbon or braid.

For flowerbeds, the background is likely to be grass, gravel or paving, enabling you to walk round instead of along as in a border. Beds can be edged with box or other neat low-growing plants, or with tiles, boards or specially made loops of wire which give the illusion that the bed is really a basket of flowers set down on the grass. 'A bed has the independence of a picture that is framed and separate' wrote Jason Hill in *The Contemplative Gardener* (1940), 'so that we can aim at more complex, subtle and strongly patterned effects than are possible in the long border, where the different colour groups must be related to their neighbours.' A single flowerbed, complete in itself, makes an ideal subject for a cushion, rug or bedspread. It can be filled with one type of flower in a single colour, or many tones of one colour, or a variety of colours and tones, and the plants can be presented individually or massed together. Elizabeth Ashurst's 'Polyanthus Bed' on page 111 was inspired by the colour harmonies and contrasts of the flowers seen from above, packed close together and set off by a deep-green tufted border.

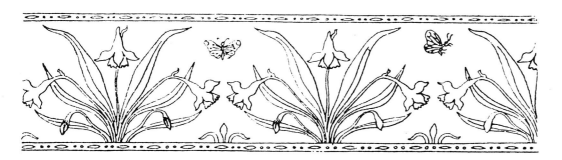

'Late Spring Garden' by Janet Haigh. Canvaswork picture of a border of tulips backed by trellis with polyanthus and pansies spilling over the brick path. The regular patterns of trellis and brick set off the random profusion of the flowers.

'Daffodils by the Gazebo, Friar Park, Henley on Thames' by Janet Galloway. Free machining, appliqué and hand stitches, mainly straight and cross, on air-brushed felt using cotton, silk and linen threads and dyed-silk strips.

'Polyanthus Bed' by Elizabeth Ashurst. Tufted border with flower heads cut out and applied with French knots.

Studies by Elizabeth Ashurst for 'Polyanthus Bed'.

Designs combining plants from the Primulaceae family based on the woodcuts of a cowslip from *La Clef des Champs* (below right) and bird's-eye primrose, scarlet pimpernel and primrose from Gerard's *Herbal*.

In botanic gardens the beds are often planted to bring together flowers of the same family, so that you can study their similarities and differences. You will find polyanthus among the Primulaceae, together with primroses, cowslips, auriculas and scarlet pimpernel whose running growth might make a border to an embroidered flowerbed designed along 'family' lines. In some botanic gardens each bed records the plant introductions of a particular period, so that you see the polyanthus with seventeenth-century plants like tradescantia, commonly known as spiderwort – a far better subject for embroidery than for the garden where it quickly overwhelms its neighbours with its strap-like leaves.

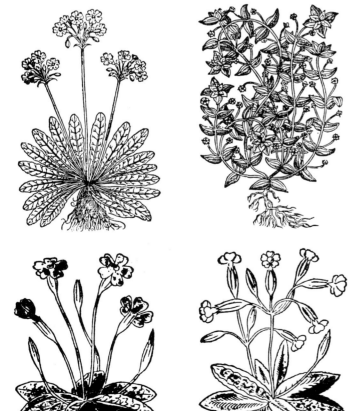

Tradescantia from Thomas Johnson's *Herball* of 1633.

Border designs based on
primroses and heartsease.

Embroiderers in the past recorded the favourite flowers of their time, together with prized new introductions, and their work also shows us the arrangements of these flowers in the garden beds and borders. To say whether contemporary garden embroidery will prove as absorbing for future historians, we have to decide which are the favourite flowers today, and this is not easy given the vast choice available. There are the 'newer', 'brighter', 'hardier' varieties competing for attention on seed packets and in plant catalogues, but at the same time there is an ever-growing interest in searching out old-fashioned flowers like the Victorian striped polyanthus and double primrose appropriate for restored nineteenth-century gardens or recreations of Elizabethan knots. Specialist nurseries stock 'unusual' plants like hostas and hellebores which appeal to flower arrangers, garden designers and embroiderers alike because of their subtle colours, beautiful leaves and interesting shapes and textures.

Texture is particularly important for embroiderers and it is especially interesting to see which flowers are noted by garden writers in terms of embroidery and fabric. Here for example is Vita Sackville-West, in 'In Your Garden' from the *Observer* of 28 May 1950, enthusing about the old-fashioned roses she loved:

> I have heard conventionally minded people remark that they like a rose to be a rose, by which they apparently mean an overblown, pink, scarlet or yellow object, desirable enough in itself, but lacking the subtlety to be found in some of those traditional roses which might be picked off a medieval tapestry or a piece of Stuart needlework. Indeed I think that you should approach them as though they were textiles rather than flowers. The velvet vermillion of the petals, the stamens of quivering gold, the slaty purple of Cardinal Richelieu, the loose dark red and gold of Alain Blanchard; I could go on for ever, but I always come back to embroidery, and of the velvet and damask with which some of them share their name.

The roses in Stuart needlework she had in mind were embroidered in detached buttonhole stitch, each petal worked separately within a loop of silk-covered wire. They are immediately recognisable as roses, just as you can tell the pinks and tulips decorating the caskets, pictures and mirror frames of the period, and they charm us because they are like, yet unlike, the real flowers. They are 'curious' in the seventeenth-century sense of the word, namely 'intriguing'. The silk petals have a textural interest of their own which does not attempt to emulate the living flowers – a sensible approach whatever the medium may be as no amount of skill can exactly reproduce the velvety sheen of a rose or pansy petal. Suggestion is always preferable to imitation, and the more you are aware of the limitations of embroidery, the easier you will find it to make these limitations work for you in adapting flowers and choosing stitches and materials to work them.

One way is to single out a particular quality of the flower you have chosen. If, for example, you are determined to bring out the velvety texture of pansy petals, you could try working them in satin stitch in lustrous thread next to grey felted stems of rose campion (*Lychnis coronaria*) and bring out their sheen by contrast. Pansies and violas have a particularly delightful way of weaving in and out of other plants, and you could exploit this habit of growth as a unifying feature of your design, repeating the flower faces in groups against the foliage of tricolour sage or golden marjoram. You might concentrate on the colour but, as Miss Jekyll noted, 'texture plays so important a part in the appearance of surface-colour that one can hardly think of colour without thinking of texture'. I saw this beautifully illustrated at the Villa Cimbrone at Ravello in southern Italy, where one compartment of the garden was planted with pansies in large separate drifts of cream, yellow, bronze, violet and blue. On entering the garden it was the mingling of these 'pansy' colours that first struck the eye, but the effect really depended on colour and texture working together. In embroidery this kind of effect works well if a single stitch – possibly tent, cross or rice stitch – is worked in drifts of colour, using two or three strands of different shades in the needle and gradually blending one drift into another. Alternatively you could piece tiny squares, hexagons or diamonds in patchwork, dyeing the fabric first in order to have a good range of tones.

'Seed Packets for impossible Gardens I' by Sarah Hosking. Coin rug hanging made from dyed cotton cut out on a fly press and then stitched by hand and machine on a cotton backing, inspired by the bright colours of the flowers printed on seed packets whose brilliance far surpasses the plants grown from them.

'Herbaceous Border at Blickling Hall, Norfolk' by Freda Waters. Miniature embroidery (3½in − 2½in) inspired by drifts of flowers and foliage freely worked in mainly straight and looped stitches with French knots on a green ground.

opposite 'Cornflowers in the Herbaceous Border' by Richard Box. The embroidery, developed from a painting, began as a fabric collage of tiny pieces of material matching the colours and tones of the original arranged to construct the shape of the entire composition by being stuck with small dabs of glue onto coloured hessian. Free machine embroidery and hand embroidery in many different colours and types of thread, contribute to the variety of textures and help to balance the colour harmonies of the design as a whole.

A design for hostas and ferns suitable for hand or machine quilting.

If you look at planting plans for beds and borders, you will see that some designers, like Miss Jekyll, use long thin drifts (see page 15), while others prefer triangular or squarish groups of plants which would obviously work well in patchwork. In a bed or border devoted to plants of a single kind, like pansies, irises or pinks, the colour alone would suggest the pansy or iris theme, and if you wanted to make it still clearer you could mark some flower heads in outline on your ground and leave them void as in Assisi work. Yet another alternative would be to take the distinctive shape of the flowers as your starting point, either the fat round faces of hybrid pansies or the delicate elongated faces of their distant ancestors, the 'heartease of the Elizabethans, strewing them at random or placing them in regular patterns as suggested in Chapter 7.

The more flowers you introduce in your borders and beds, the more careful must be your planning. Describing the richness and profusion of the planting at Hidcote in Gloucestershire, Vita Sackville-West wrote: 'What I should like to impress upon the reader is the luxuriance everywhere; a kind of haphazard luxuriance, which of course comes neither by hap nor by hazard at all.' Though happy accidents happen in needlework – like the self-sown plants that find perfect positions for themselves in the garden – really memorable embroidery does not come by hap or by

hazard either, but by working the scheme out carefully and choosing appropriate methods and materials. Only then can you stitch freely, balancing the colours, textures and shapes to create a needlework equivalent of the luxuriant, apparently informal 'cottage garden' planting that is the keynote in gardens like Hidcote, Sissinghurst and Great Dixter.

In the real garden, beds and borders should look effective as a whole seen from a distance and near-to when the beauty of the grouping and the individual plants is revealed. In embroidery you can choose your viewpoint and take advantage of the garden designer's skill, knowing that his or her aim in creating harmonies of colour and textural interest is identical to your own. Russell Page likens the planning process to 'weaving a herbaceous tapestry; building plant by plant and variety by variety a texture valid at any point, as you have considered the shape and colour of each plant in relation to its neighbours'. He suggests working out the scheme first in monochrome, balancing the areas of dark and light, of lustrous and matt foliage, and this is equally sound advice when you plan an embroidery design.

You might begin with a happy marriage of ferns and hostas, an all-green scheme providing dramatic contrast of form and texture. In selecting which of the many varieties of each plant would transpose well in embroidery you will

Designs for cushions based on the delicate sweet violet and the round-faced pansy.

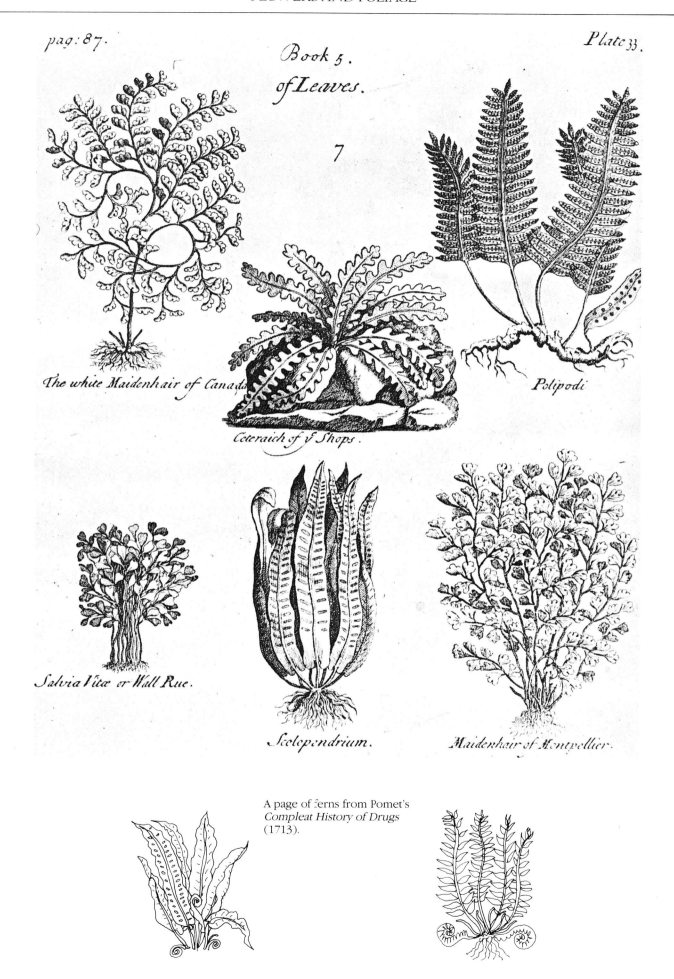

Book 5.
of Leaves.

7

Plate 33.

The white Maidenhair of Canada

Ceteraich of ỹ Shops.

Polipodi

Salvia Vitæ or Wall Rue.

Scolopendrium.

Maidenhair of Montpellier.

A page of ferns from Pomet's *Compleat History of Drugs* (1713).

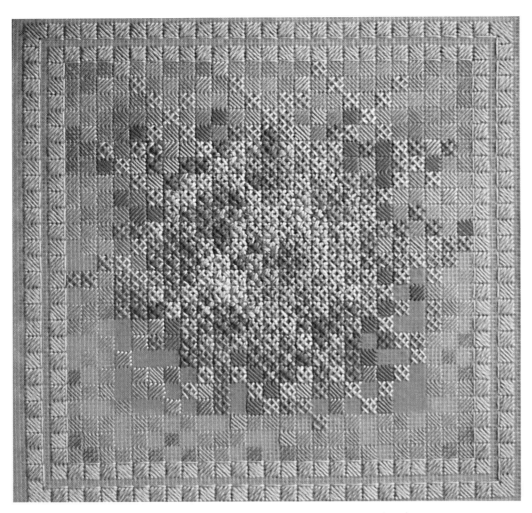

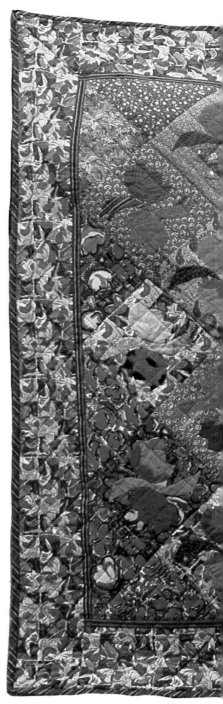

'Precious Garden' by Vicky Lugg. Canvaswork inspired by harmonies of pink and red flowers growing side by side. Rice and flat stitches on gauze-covered canvas together create a subtly luminous effect.

discover unsuspected intricacies of pattern suitable for working out in crewelwork, quilting, free stitchery, machine embroidery and on canvas. Choose the method that appeals to you most and then assemble the shades of green you think appropriate. 'For your embroidery-palette certain definite sets of green will be necessary', wrote May Morris in *Decorative Needlework* (1893), 'full, pure yellow green, greyish green and blue green, two or three shades of each.' If you plan to use threads of different textures and thickness, try putting them together on your ground to assess their effect. Seeing them juxtaposed may suggest the addition of some light lime green as in the haze of minute flowers hovering above the velvety leaves of lady's mantle (*Alchemilla mollis*), in which case you must rearrange and rebalance your design.

This experience of designing and working a group is I think invaluable when one embarks on a scheme using more colours and shapes. The game you play of 'put and take', moving reels and hanks of thread on your ground, is the needlework equivalent to trying out new plant associations by digging up clumps and resiting them having tried out the effect first with cut flowers and foliage. On garden visits the sight of a discreet label with the message 'move to left of lilac' means that the gardener is engaged in the endless and fascinating pursuit of refining the garden picture. This you can do in stitchery, adding a touch of vivid pink to bring out the intensity of the blues, or a hint of sunlit sparkle in a needleful of metallic thread.

'Tulip Bed' by Dieuwke
Philpott. Quilt with tulip heads
applied in tones of pink and
red.

Tulips drawn by John Farleigh
in *Old Fashioned Flowers* by
Sacheverell Sitwell.

Chapter heading from *The Art and Craft of Garden Making*, with a pretty leaf border.

below Flowers with distinctive shapes make good subjects for embroidery. From left to right the stitches suggested are French knots, cretan, fly and detached chain.

I suggested you start with a bold group of foliage plants because leaves are often easier to simplify than flowers. In garden and embroidery they provide focal points and balance the less distinct outlines of nearby plants. Compare the many different shapes of hosta foliage with other large-leaved plants like shiny bergenias, intricately pleated veratrum and melianthus and finely cut hellebores. Leaves can be spotted, striped, marbled and blotched, as well simply or intricately veined. The leaf shapes of some trees suggest their outline when they are fully grown, and this simplification may lead you to choose a method such as appliqué, inlay or patchwork. If you study trees in winter you will appreciate their skeletal shapes, some round, some flat topped, some upright, and some with layered or weeping branches. The old but true adage that you should look out for the shapes *between* the branches in embroidery design was brought home to me most clearly by the practical experience of pruning out old wood to create a well-shaped tree or shrub.

Clear uncluttered shapes transpose best in stitchery, and it is worthwhile noting and grouping together for reference and future association plants you find particularly striking. Spire-like flowers are always eye-catching, whether they are solid and stately, like delphiniums and foxgloves, or light and elegant like foxtail lilies. Vita Sackville-West recommended contrasting 'monuments of solidity' like stocks and phlox with 'see through flowers' like plume poppies, thalictrum and clouds of gypsophila. Note how individual

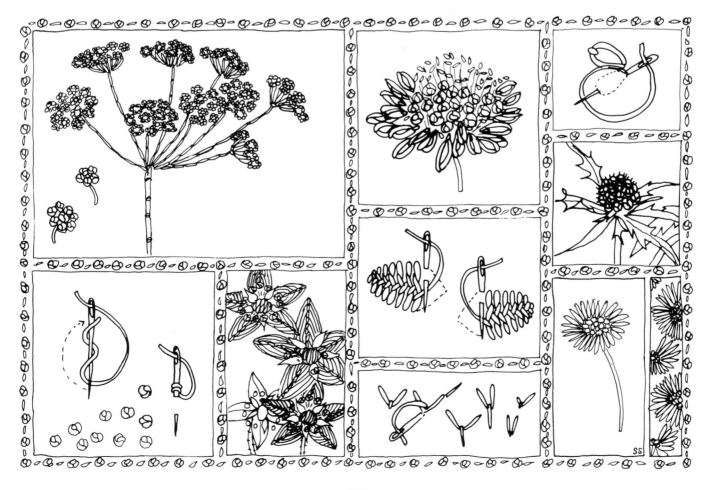

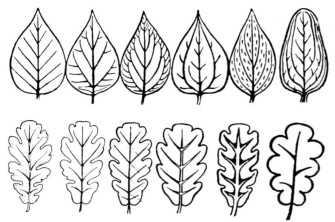

The veining of leaves suggests different decorative treatments, drawn here by Ralph Hatton.

flowers clothe the spire to form further patterns as in the closely set stars of the yellow asphodel and *Sisyrinchium striatum*. Star shapes are particularly satisfying to work, either on canvas in cross, Algerian and star eyelets or in free stitchery in ermine, crossed fly, back-stitched star, spider's web or crossed stitches tied with tiny cross stitch at the centre. Star-shaped flowers vary in scale from the minute pointed blooms of pratia, to the close carpeting of chiono-doxa (glory of the snow) in spring, and the great globular heads of *Allium albopilosum* made up of eighty separate violet stars. Flowers with distinctive stamens – hypericums, astrantias and cranesbills – create similar decorative effects.

'Correspondence in General Contour between Leaf and Tree' from *Line and Form* by Walter Crane (1900).

'Various leaf forms' from *Progressive Design for Students* by James Ward (1902).

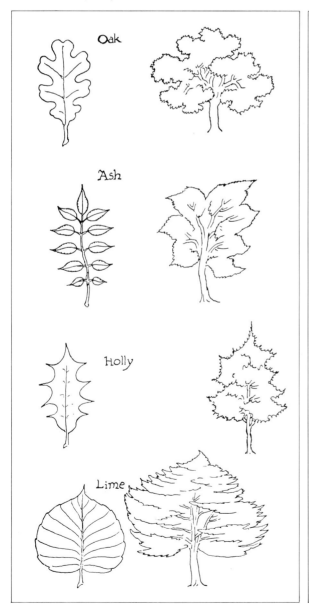

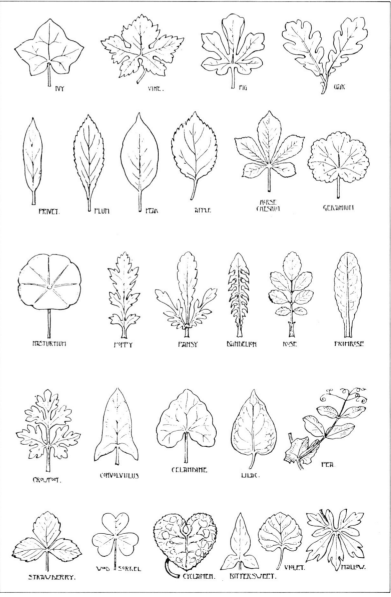

Formalised flower designs from
Drawing Design and Craftwork
by F. S. Glass (1920).

Cowslip design from
Progressive Design for Students
by J. Ward (1902).

Plants with rigid branching stems like tall *Verbena bonariensis* and sea holly (Eryngium) call for looped stitches such as feather and Cretan. Almost all the varieties of eryngium are exciting subjects for embroidery; their angular and spikey qualities make them suitable for canvaswork, while the ruffs framing the flower heads (*Eryngium planum* and *E. alpinum* especially) are reminiscent of needle lace. You could exploit the branching structure of these tall 'see through' plants to frame small-scale garden views. Think of the decorative arched frames which could be made using the curving stems of solomon's seal (*Polygonatum multiflorum*) and angel's fishing rods (*Dierama pendulum*).

Radial shapes, whether they are ruffs as in celandines and love-in-the-mist; petals as in cornflowers, marigolds and daisies, or basal rosettes, as in London pride, repay the closest observation, especially if you choose a high view-point.

Many of the flowers in my garden were chosen because they fascinated me as possible subjects for embroidery. This year, considerations of viewpoint made me experiment with flat-growing plants which grow as rugs, mats and pillows. Also, inspired by Vita Sackville-West I am trying out low-growing alpines of 'the sorts that make little tufts and squabs and cushions and pools of colour when in flower, and neat tight bumps of grey or green for the rest of the year when the flowers have gone'. I have planted silene, thrift, acaenas, houseleeks and thyme with violas and clumps of dianthus, and this winter hope to use the experience gained in choosing and juxtaposing them to design and work a cushion recording my pleasure in seeing and tending them. The experiment may be a failure, but so far everything about it has been absorbing; and when it comes to the embroidery, I feel sure it will give the 'delight and refreshment of mind' which Gertrude Jekyll considered the best purpose of a garden.

Primrose border from Miss
Higgin's *Handbook of
Embroidery* (1912).

'Dreamed Garden – not the summer of '86' by Paddy Ramsay. Picture in free-machine quilting and appliqué in satins and velvets. The bold leaves of the hostas in the foreground are strikingly defined by this method.

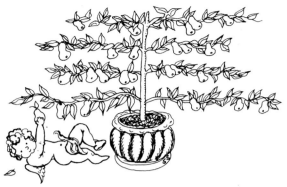

9

HERBS, VEGETABLES AND FRUIT

'And as for the other quarters set out with beds of floures and sweet smelling herbs, what reckoning was made of them in the old time may appear by this, that a man could not heretofore come by a commoner's house within the citie, but he should see the windows beautified with green quishins [cushions] wrought [embroidered] and tapissied [woven] with floures of all colours, resembling daily to their view, the Gardens indeed which were in the out-villages, as being in the very heart of the citie, they might think themselves in the countrey.'

Natural History, Pliny, 1st century AD
(translated by Philemon Holland)

The green cushions embroidered in the first century to remind city dwellers of plots of flowers and 'poignant hearbes' in country gardens are the distant ancestors of those illustrated in this book. It is fascinating to find proof of the tradition for recording garden pleasures reaching so far back into antiquity. The Roman embroiderers of Pliny's day would have had many different herbs to choose from. Most are sun-lovers which flourish in the Mediterranean, and the Romans grew them extensively for dyeing, culinary, medicinal and cosmetic purposes. The Romans were also skilled in the cultivation of fruit and vegetables, and introduced many new food crops to Britain. Some of these may have died out in the Dark Ages following the collapse of the Roman Empire, though medieval embroidered vestments record the vines they established. It was not until the Tudor period that a wide range of herbs, vegetables and fruit was again available.

Elizabethan and Jacobean embroidery provides a fascinating commentary on the decorative way many of these plants were grown. Although some writers distinguished between 'nosegay gardens' and 'gardens of herbs', there was clearly considerable overlapping with the herbs grown ornamentally to outline the knots (see Chapter 5), vegetables like runner beans grown on arbours, and fruits like wild strawberries creeping in everywhere, just as they do today. An intriguing record survives at Hardwick Hall in Derbyshire in the shape of a set of small octagonal panels worked in tent stitch in wool and silk. They were mounted on a screen in the nineteenth century, but originally they were worked either as trenchers (the Elizabethan form of table mat), or, more probably, for application to wall or bed

hangings like the famous panels mounted on green velvet at Oxburgh Hall in Norfolk. They were based on woodcuts in a herbal by the Italian Matthioli and they bear the initials of Bess of Hardwick, the most celebrated embroiderer of her day.

How satisfying it would be to know which of the vegetables and other plants Bess embroidered were actually grown by her at Hardwick; but though everything inside the house was recorded in the great inventory of 1601, no mention was made of the garden and its contents. Nevertheless, one of the pleasures of visiting Hardwick today is to walk in the extensive herb garden laid out by the National Trust, and to study the plants and compare them with their embroidered counterparts on the furnishings inside the house. The background on the 'Pear Tree' long cushion opposite, for example, is covered with slips of flowers and fruit including grapes on a vine which can be traced back to *La Clef des Champs* by Jacques le Moyne de Morgues, published in 1586. This charming tiny volume, with its woodcuts of herbs, vegetables and fruit, was intended as a pattern book for embroiderers and craftsmen of all kinds – painters, jewellers, tapestry weavers and sculptors. Many of its motifs (see page 138) are as appealing for use in garden embroidery today as they were four centuries ago. You could use them to devise an orchard or potager (where herbs, vegetables and fruit are grown ornamentally together), arranging them in pairs as le Moyne did, or set them within the interlace of a knot or as a border. They would be equally charming worked in tent stitch, cross stitch or long and short, or outlined in couching or machine whip stitch for cushions or place mats.

The 'Pear Tree', a long cushion at Hardwick Hall embroidered with slips of fruit and flowers. The grape motif below was based on this woodcut from *La Clef des Champs* (1586).

A pictorial plan of an ornamental vegetable garden from Leonard Meager's *New Art of Gardening* (1697).

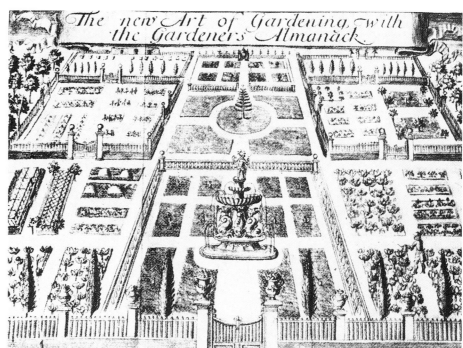

The new Art of Gardening, with the Gardener's Almanack

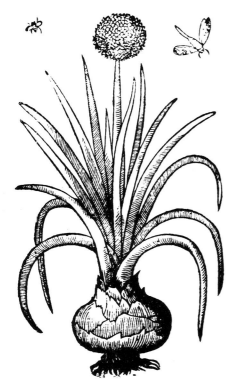

Woodcut of an onion used as a pattern in a small octagonal panel at Hardwick Hall, and a contemporary treatment of the design.

Le Moyne depicted borage with its intense cerulean petals and distinctive black eye. This was a favourite in gardens and embroidery, appearing on every conceivable item of dress and furnishing. It was still popular in the seventeenth century when John Parkinson included it in the flower section of his *Paradisi in Sole Paradisus Terrestris, The Garden of Pleasant Flowers* (1629) rather than among the vegetables because it was so often chosen as a motif in needlework. Parkinson's book is well worth perusing today for further motifs of herbs, vegetables and fruit, all of which are most strikingly presented, with the details of their structure boldly defined. In his time, as with the Elizabethans before him, the distinction between 'herbs' and 'vegetables' was not so clear as it is now, and the vegetable aspect of the herb garden did not seem to him the most appealing, even if it was immensely useful. He insists that the 'herb garden should be on the one or other side of the house . . . for the different scents that arise from the herbs, as cabbages, onions etc are scarce well pleasing to perfume the lodgings of any house'.

By the eighteenth century, the walled enclosure of the kitchen garden was usually removed even further from the house, and clear plans in Batty Langley's *New Principles of Gardening* (1728) show how it was arranged with fruit trained on the walls and neat regular beds. The stippling, minute dots and dashes and circles on the plans look remarkably like an indication of simple stitches. If the beds were outlined in couching and the plants were worked in running stitches, French knots, speckling and detached chain stitches, this would be a simple pattern for beginners. But it is also reminiscent of blackwork, for which more complex filling stitches could be worked out. Batty Langley listed the 'herbs as are absolutely necessary for the service of all Gentlemen and their Families in general' and he wrote their names on the plan. This adds to its interest and appeal, and is an idea worth considering in an embroidered version. If, however, you decided to pursue this theme, you would have to re-space the lettering to make sure it contributed to the effectiveness of your design, and did not unbalance it.

John Parkinson's illustration of borage included in *Paradise in Sole Paradisus Terrestris* because it was a favourite motif for needlework.

'Highfield Nurseries Ornamental Fruit Garden' by Pam Watts, made to celebrate the gold medal (top centre) won by the owners of the nursery at the Chelsea Flower Show in 1984. The design follows the plan closely, interpreting it imaginatively on canvas with flat- or mosaic-stitch paving, Ghiordes-knot box edgings and the fruit tunnel of cordon apple and pears trained on hoops seen from above as rows of tufting over a 'path' of narrow strips laid and painted to match the canvas ground. The rich textured embroidery of herbs, vegetables and fruit grown ornamentally echoes the decorative appeal of the real garden.

Highfield Nurseries' plan for the Chelsea Flower Show garden on which Pam Watts based her embroidery.

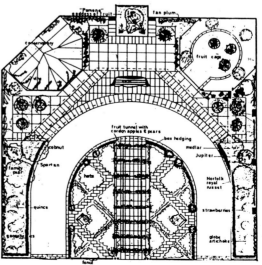

127

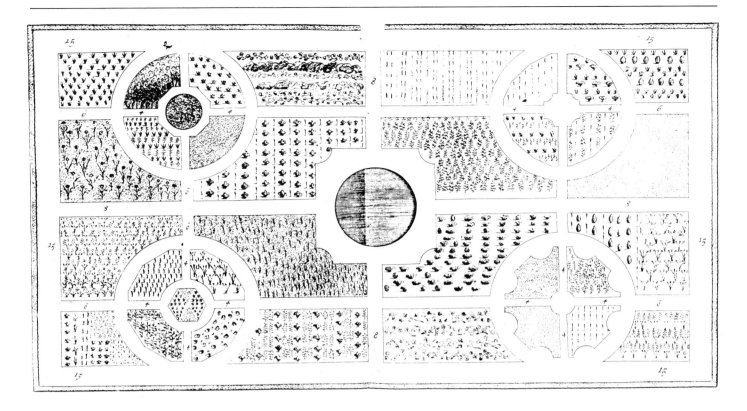

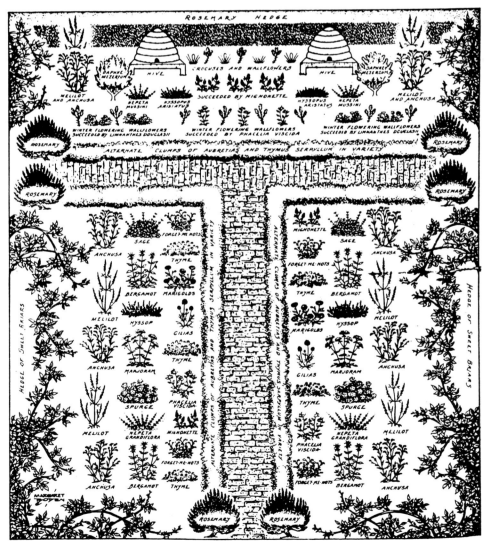

The vegetable-garden plan from Batty Langley's *New Principles of Gardening* resembles machine embroidery.

opposite Another kitchen-garden plan from *New Principles of Gardening* suitable for simple running or detached stitches (the Lindley Library).

Herb garden plan from Eleanour Sinclair Rohde's nursery catalogue.

It is interesting to compare Batty Langley's plan with the pictorial design from the 1943 catalogue of Eleanour Sinclair Rohde's nursery where each plant in the symmetrical arrangement is named and drawn in profile. Eleanour Sinclair Rohde was a fine practical gardener as well as a noted authority on historical gardens, as is apparent in the plan where she has selected herbs to be compatible in scale and structure. She has not included any invasive thugs like fennel or mint, giants like lovage or angelica or stragglers like sage which so disrupt the gardener's attempts to create a formal herb garden. In embroidery of course this does not matter, you can work either a perspective or vertical viewpoint and choose the herbs for their subtle colours, shapes and decorative appeal.

If you feel unsure about your handling of colour in garden embroidery, a herb garden is a good subject for experiment. Begin using only shades of green with acid green for golden marjoram and feverfew, bright greens for young chives, blue green for rue, richer darker greens for parsley and duller shades for sage. If you add shades of soft yellow in the flowers of fennel and lovage the effect will still be harmonious, but if you add vivid marigolds or nasturtiums these will contrast with the greens and focus your attention on their brightness. Blend herbs with soft mauve, pinkish and purplish flowers such as chives, hyssop, lavender and sage and see how well they look together, then see how their tones alter when you introduce brighter notes in the clear red of bergamot or the blue of borage. You can work the herbs in a single stitch relying on subtlety of tone for your effect, or you can formalize their shapes and reduce them all to the same size as Doris Tomlinson and Genny Morrow have done on page 131. In their embroidered herb garden the angular nature of canvaswork is appreciated and exploited to brilliant advantage. Many herbs like fennel, lovage, southernwood and rue, have interesting structures which could be developed in free stitchery in looped stitches; Cretan, feather and fly are the most obvious. Other herbs, such as oregano or low-growing thymes, spread out to cover the ground in dense mats which could be built up in French knots or worked in coral or scroll stitch.

Because of the current revival of interest in herb growing, many beautiful gardens devoted to them have been laid out in recent years. Visit as many as you can, compare the designs and plant associations, and look with a selective eye to see which arrangements would work best in embroidery. The simplest kind of formal design – a chequerboard of alternating square paving stones and herbs designed by Eleanour Sinclair Rohde at Lullingstone in Kent, or the five-circle plan made in 1907 by Gertrude Jekyll for Knebworth House in Hertfordshire and recently executed – is often the most effective. The strong simple design both separates and sets off the herbs. One of the best-loved and most effective plans looks back to the medieval cloister, where the square or rectangular space within the walls and arcading was divided into regular beds by paths, with small hedges round each of the beds. At the centre was a focal point in the shape of a well-head, sundial or fountain. Two of the most lovely herb gardens in England, at Sissinghurst in Kent and Cranborne Manor in Dorset, follow this plan. Each lies some way from the main garden and is enclosed by yew hedges so that it is secluded, peaceful and wonderfully refreshing to both mind and eye. The fragrance, the muted colours, and the feeling that you have somehow gone back in time, all add to the enchantment.

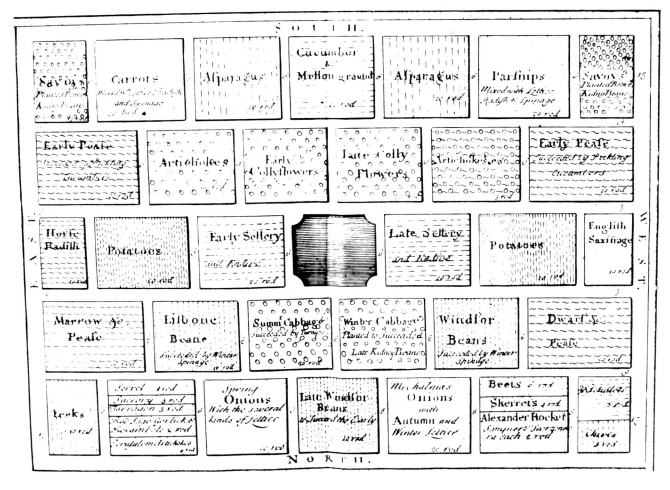

'Herb Garden' by Margaret Rivers. Small pieces of frayed transparent material were applied to a painted calico ground with simple straight stitches. In the foreground, bright orange marigolds in buttonhole stitch contrast with the muted tones of the taller herbs.

'Herb Garden' by Sylvia Bramley. The garden is enclosed within a lavender border of fine wool worked in three rows of overlapping herringbone stitch cut through and 'stones' in French knots in silk.

'Herb Garden' by Doris Tomlinson and Genny Morrow reflects the designers' interest in the traditional patterns of American patchwork. Thirty-nine different canvas stitches are ingeniously combined including a cashmere variation stitch using pen-wiped wool for the brick walk, slanted Gobelin stitch in an ombré technique to give a misty effect to the sage flowers and an alicia lace variation stitch for the leaves.

Design based on the five-circle herb garden at Knebworth.

Designs combining herbal motifs from the florilegium below with knots in the herb gardens at Moseley Old Hall and Little Moreton Hall. These could be used for place mats or cushions.

opposite Fruit protected by frames, and cloches and bell jars set out neatly in an illustration from *New Improvements of Planting and Gardening* by Richard Bradley (1726).

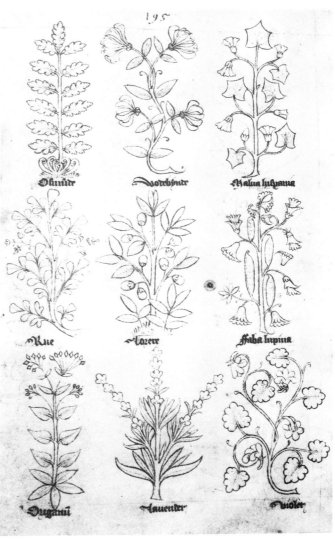

A page of decoratively drawn medicinal plants including rue, lavender, mallow and honeysuckle from a mid-fifteenth-century florilegium in the British Library.

Designs based on the florilegium.

Another herb garden which would transpose well in embroidery can be seen at Little Moreton Hall in Cheshire. Here a knot has been set out following Leonard Meager's plan in *The Complete Gardener* of 1670. The design is laid out in box, bordered on two sides by wide herb beds with the varieties neatly set out in squares. You could follow this design, simplifying the knot and filling the squares with a single plant or sprig to indicate the varieties as suggested on page 132.

A similar treatment combining a bird's-eye view and plant portraits would be equally successful in the vegetable garden where the symmetrical layout of beds separated by paths, their edges outlined by box, planks or a line of tiles, has been unchanged for centuries. Here is another cornucopia of designs for the embroiderer: the sampler-like patterns of seedlings and rows of regularly spaced vegetables, the exciting contrast of glowing reds and greens in the stems of ruby chard or purple podded beans, the eye-catching shapes of artichokes and rhubarb, and the solid forms of piled up flowerpots and barrow by the potting shed. A kitchen garden, secluded and well ordered is a delight, and many gardeners would share Joseph Addison's enthusiasm when he wrote in the *Spectator* in 1712:

> I have always thought a Kitchin-garden a more pleasant sight than the finest Orangery or artifial Greenhouse. I love to see every Thing in its perfection, and am more pleased to survey my rows of Coleworts and Cabbages, with a thousand nameless Potherbs, springing up in their full Fragrancy and Verdure, than to see the tender Plants of foreign countries kept alive by artificial Heats.

Despite the regular rows of coleworts and cabbages, Addison's garden was a 'confusion of Kitchin and Parterre, Orchard and Flower Garden, mixt and interwoven with one another' so that it looked like a natural wilderness. 'Luxuriancy and Profusion' were the keynotes, but the whole scheme was still carefully planned in that plants flowering at the same season were arranged 'to compose a picture of great Variety'. The effect must have resembled the miscellany of fruit, flowers, herbs and vegetables we might find in a country cottage garden. It would have been closely similar to that achieved in this century at Hidcote Manor and Barnsley House in Gloucestershire where our first impression is of this joyous 'Luxuriancy and Profusion'. Should you want to transpose this rich and varied planting into embroidery, try the tracing-paper method and concentrate on defining the shapes and tones of a small area. If there are bean poles or panels of netting, their strong verticals and criss-cross patterns may be useful in strengthening your design.

Indeed you could make the grid established by panels of netting, either the bright green plastic type or the old-fashioned black kind, a feature of your design for the square and diamond patterns of the mesh contrast with the natural growth of the plants it supports or protects from birds. It is pleasing whether it is set vertically between posts for sweet peas, beans and so on, spread horizontally over low-growing crops like strawberries, or draped over flowering or fruiting trees trained against a wall. Imagine an espalier cherry tree trained on a mellow brick wall, and netted over with emerald-green mesh, giving a complex effect of pattern on pattern to explore. You could print the brick pattern with a simple block, and use herringbone or wave stitches for the mesh in the finest possible threads. Try milliner's net over a collage of cut leaf shapes, or cut up a coloured net bag in which fruit is sold. The branching pattern of the fruit tree could be defined in looped or outline stitches.

'Radish' bag designed by Sara Midda and reminiscent of her exquisite illustrations in *In and Out of the Garden*. It was worked by her mother, Evelyn Davis, in tent stitch.

'Rabbit in a Cabbage Bed' by Belinda Pollit. Trapunto quilting on silk organza, the rabbit stuffed with snippets of silk thread and outlined in back stitch, the beetroot leaves in needlewoven space-dyed thread, and the cabbages in applied pieces of stitched patterned silk.

'Economical Layout of a Kitchen Garden' from *How to make your Garden Grow* by Heath Robinson and K. R. G. Browne.

135

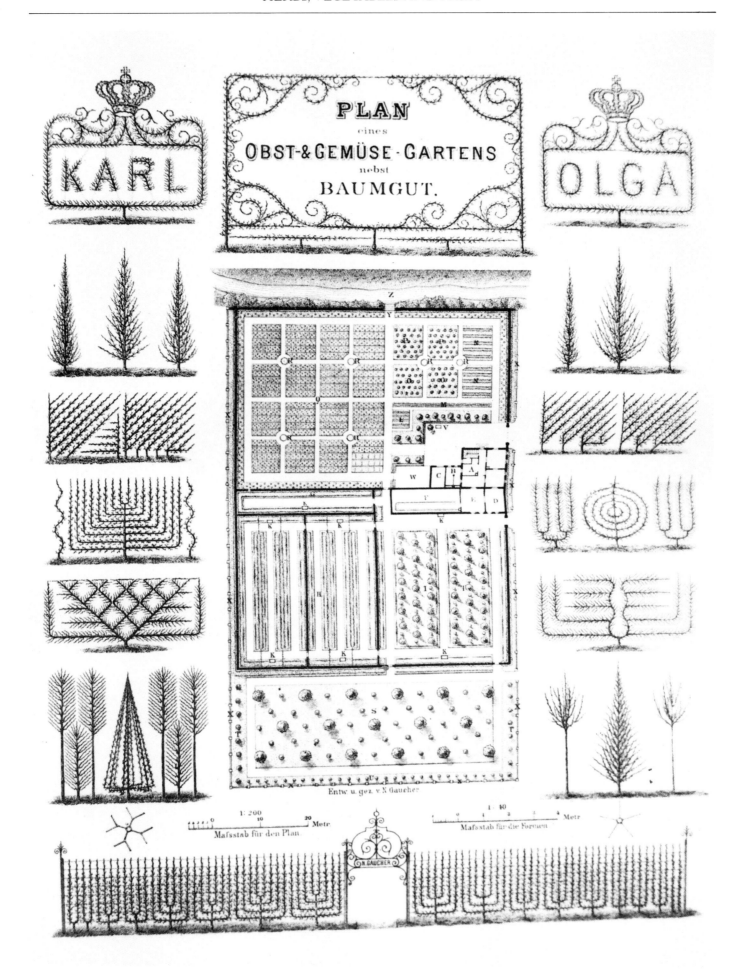

opposite Fruit trees trained into an amazing variety of shapes from the fruit manual of Nicolas Gaucher (1902). Their angular forms suggest blackwork or canvas stitches.

The training and pruning of fruit trees to promote good crops and easy picking is a tradition going back to the Romans, and the effect is highly decorative. Whether grown in orchards, against walls, or planted as living screens or tunnels, the trees look equally beautiful in flower and fruit. Fruit trees have always been a favourite motif in the embroiderer's garden. Diminutive stumpy trees bearing crops of giant fruit with eager birds perching in the branches are a feature of Renaissance canvaswork and seventeenth-century stumpwork, and reflect the interest in fruit growing and grafting at the time. Today's embroiderers might follow this tradition, inspired by the recently introduced 'step over' fruit trees whose branches are trained horizontally at a low level to form borders in ornamental vegetable gardens and potagers. As we have so often seen, the vertical viewpoint provides inspiration for embroidery, and here the delicate blossom or ripe fruit clustering along the branches form attractive and unusual frames for the individual beds. The distinctive shape of pears set off by pointed leaves would be particularly effective as a border worked in quilting or appliqué on a cushion.

During the nineteenth century the training of fruit trees into ever more unusual and fanciful shapes became a craze, which must have tested the skill and imagination of many a head gardener. Peaches and pears were trained to form the initials or name of the owner of the garden, and apples and soft fruit such as gooseberries and currants were trained in an amazing variety of shapes providing ready-made patterns which could be developed in canvaswork, blackwork or free stitching.

Monogram formed of trained peach and pear trees illustrated in William Robinson's *Parks, Promenades and Gardens of Paris* (1869).

Three fruit trees by Walter Crane from *Line and Form* (1900)

Detail of a vegetable garden by Margaret Rochester combining a plan with plants seen in elevation.

Fruit and vegetable motifs from *La Clef des Champs* (1586).

opposite 'Rhubarb' by Fiona Rainford based on a drawing of rhubarb which had gone to seed. Free stitchery on a sprayed ground, with further spraying and painting on the applied leather. Some of the threads were also space dyed to create subtle graduations in tone.

10

WATER GARDENS

'Water in the garden whether pond or stream, lakeside or artificial pool, offers the gardener temptations hard to resist. Before your inner eye float luscious pictures of groups of iris and primula, willows and water lilies and a mirage of picturesque details culled from books and exhibition catalogues. Too much enthusiasm of this kind and you may quite likely damage your garden composition irretrievably . . . My thought is always "How little can I do?", rather than how much, to achieve the most telling result.'

Russell Page, *The Education of a Gardener*

Garden and embroidery enthusiasts would do well to take Russell Page's warning to heart, for water, symbol of life and purity, is a feature which focuses the attention and draws the eye more compellingly than any other, making errors of scale and suitability horribly apparent. Water is tempting in both the real garden and in embroidery because it can be used in such a variety of ways and suggest such widely different moods. Moving water, rising in foaming spires from fountain jets or tumbling down in cascades, refreshes and invigorates, putting us in a carefree festive mood. Still water, dark and mysterious or mirroring images of sky and garden in lakes, canals and pools evokes a more contemplative state of mind.

Anyone who explores the fountain features at Versailles before they are turned on will note a change in mood from calmness, sometimes tinged with sadness, to exhilaration and excitement when the columns of water rise up, arch and fall in foam and ripples on the surface of the basins and fountain figures. Describing their spellbinding qualities in 1709 the French garden writer d'Argenville found:

Fountains and waterworks are the life of the garden; these make the principal ornament of it, and which animate and invigorate it, and, if I may say so, give it life and spirit. 'Tis certain, that a garden, be it in other respects never so fine, if it wants water, appears dull and melancholy, and is deficient in one of its greatest beauties.

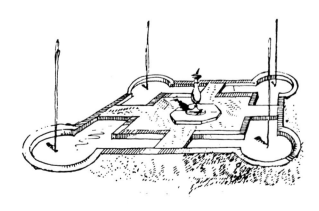

Two perspective sketches for simple water gardens from *Gardens for Small Country Houses* by Gertrude Jekyll and Lawrence Weaver (1912).

Fountain patterns from M. Boitard's *l'Architecte des Jardins* (1845).

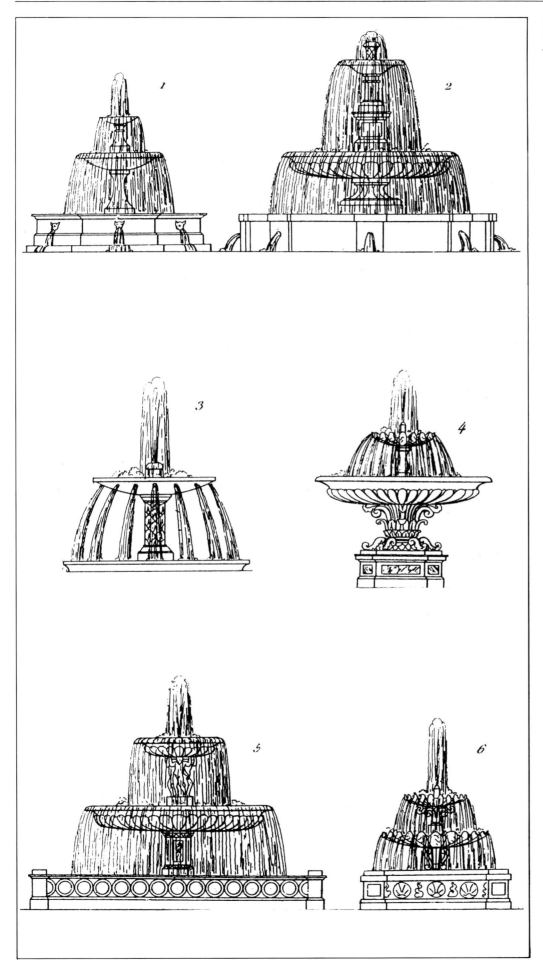

'Topiary Reflections' by Janet Haigh. Canvaswork picture using stranded cottons pulled apart and reblended.

opposite Detail from 'Moon and Watercarriers' by Belinda Downes. The water pouring from the vase held by the fountain figure of Pisces reveals the shapes of fish worked in satin stitch. The figure is padded and the ground is dyed muslin, shadow quilted with carded wools.

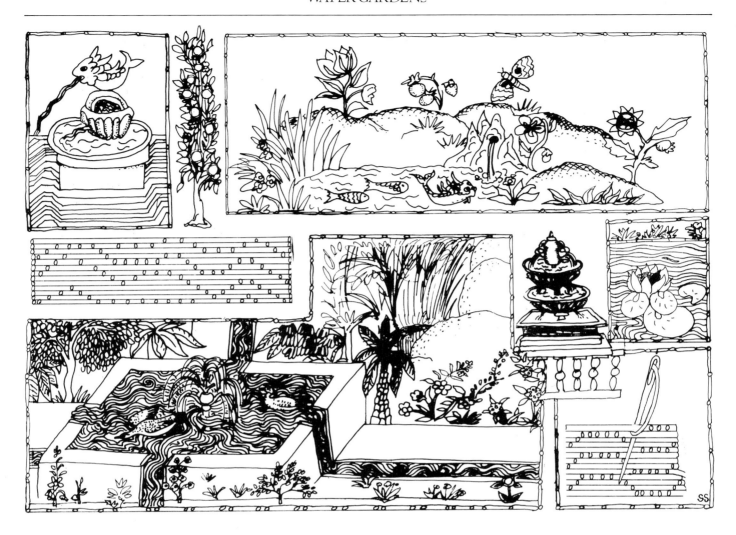

The water patterns in the stumpwork pools and in channels and 'chadars' in Persian and Mughal miniatures are full of suggestions for stitchery. Laid work in which long strands of thread are loosely laid on the surface of the material and held down by further patterns in couching is quick to do and effective in glossy and shaded threads.

Even in the smallest garden a single bubbling jet or a tiny gleaming pool can animate the scene and create magical effects in sunlight. The patterns are endlessly fascinating, changing as they do from moment to moment. To transpose these effects into embroidery is a challenge, and will only succeed if considerable thought is given to the design and stitches which will interpret them. The closest observation of water patterns in the real garden and in paintings and photographs is essential. Remember Claude Monet's scores of studies of the pool and water lilies at Giverny. The 'subject' is, we might think, always the same; but each version differs. The surface of the water, the lilies, the overhanging willow branches and the sky and clouds above are freshly observed, seen in endlessly different moments of calm or slight wind, sunshine or twilight, movement or repose.

Equally important is the study of methods used by embroiderers in the past to depict water, for example the fountain pools of seventeenth-century stumpwork. Here a quite astonishing variety of small-scale patterns is worked in coloured silks in Gobelin, Hungarian, diagonal and many other stitches to suggest the movement of water in the streams and rock-ringed fountain pools. Compare this intricacy with the extreme simplicity of the undulating lines of couched wool which symbolically but so convincingly convey the idea of swift-running water in the Bayeux Tapestry. Look again at the woven Persian garden carpet on page 42 and see how the strictly formalized water patterns succeed in creating the impression of movement.

Stitch ideas for a water garden, based on a Mughal miniature, showing a formal layout with water channels and a 'chadar' or chute.

'Persian Water Garden' by Sue Bakker. Miniature rug, 6in square, worked in stranded cottons with iridescent thread added in the central pool.

opposite 'A Persian Flower Garden' by Grace Christie. This was the frontispiece to *Samplers and Stitches* when it first appeared in 1920.

Persian water gardens often incorporated decorative stonework like these pietra-dura panels made for the Taj Mahal.

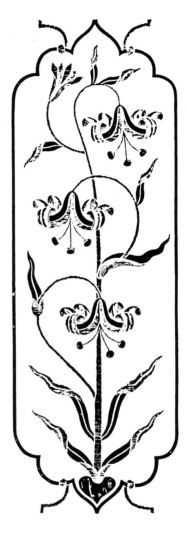

The whole design of the traditional Persian garden is related to the Biblical and Koranic presentation of Paradise, out of which four rivers – usually quartering the garden itself like irrigation channels – flow out from the centre of the garden in which, more often than not, a central pavilion is placed over the source and meeting of the four streams. The Mughal emperors took up this idea both in their garden carpets, and in their gardens, finding more and more ways to bring out the importance of water – the lifegiving element in a dry and dusty land. They made raised tanks, so that the mirroring water patterns could be enjoyed closer to eye level, and from these still tanks decorative chutes (chadars) carved with ridged wave designs led the water in a foaming, chattering rush down to more pools and channels. The word 'chadar' means a shawl, and the glistening water eddying over the stone waves must indeed have resembled the soft floating folds of the ladies' silk and muslin shawls, exquisitely embroidered, and worn with such grace in the Mughal miniatures. How interesting to find a similar image in England a century later, in Batty Langley's *New Principles of Gardening* (1728), where a cascade

> Runs down a polished Rock; and as it flows,
> Like Linen in the Air expanded shows,
> The Textile Flood a slender current holds,
> And in a wavy Veil the Place infolds.

What an inspiration for an experiment in free smocking, pleating and irregularly spacing the folds of a fine white material, and holding them down with detached stitches to form subsidiary patterns! Continuous lines of machine quilting on silk would also be tempting, as they might suggest the undulating surface of the stone over which the water moves.

In Mughal gardens shallow stone basins, some square, some round, some octagonal, and some carved in the shape of open flowers (even showing the separate petals) were animated by the play from a small central fountain-jet which sent the water running over the ridged surface in eddying patterns. It is worth stressing that many of these designs, both in carpets and in miniature paintings, are conceived as if seen from above vertically, or with a simplified naïve perspective which brings you back again and again to a vertical representation of part of the water scheme.

Sue Bakker's 'Persian Water Garden' was evolved after studying the garden carpets and the sophisticated water effects recorded in them. Her shallow pool is square, and she uses just two shades of blue stranded cotton to trace the streams of water gushing from the central source and spreading over the complex network of the stone basin. The

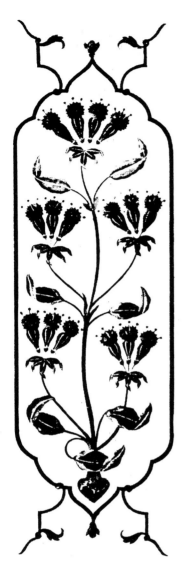

Flat patterns of inlaid coloured stones from the Taj Mahal which might be adapted as bookmarker or border designs.

Formalized treatment of water
and roots in a woodcut of iris in
the Latin *Herbarius* (1499).

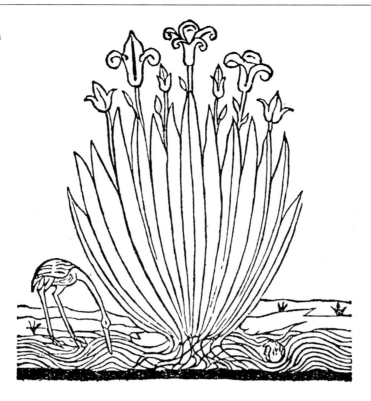

Waterlilies and plantain from
the herbals of John Gerard and
Matthioli.

149

variations in the whirls and eddies of the water patterns as they move out towards the straight edges of the pool contrast with the regular patterns framing it. These in their turn evoke the real flowers and the formalised plants inlaid in coloured stone in buildings like the Taj Mahal in India. The 'Persian Water Garden' is worked entirely in tent stitch, and it is interesting to compare the effect with the variety of different stitches in the 'Persian Flower Garden' worked by Grace Christie in 1920 on handmade linen. Here the flowers, birds, insects and animals are in cross stitch, their delicate outlines contrasting with the solid filling of wave stitch in the central pool, and the straight Gobelin in the outer channel has the effect of emphasizing the water features and coordinating the design.

In 'Topiary Reflections', Janet Haigh also chooses even-weave, but the design is based on a perspective view rather than a plan, and the water in the formal pool is still rather than in movement, reflecting an inverted mirror image of the topiary birds on the battlemented hedge. This is a classic composition, a perfectly balanced garden picture, serene yet somehow mysterious. Christopher Hussey in an article 'The Place of Ornament in the Garden' (1929) in the *RHS Journal* wrote:

> The most moving aspect of water is in its still reflections. Regarding a pool as an ever changing picture, its frame should be left as plain as possible. Where there are plenty of high things for it to reflect its basin should be brimfull.

In 'Topiary Reflections', a grass verge provides the frame to the brimfull pool and contrasts of texture and tone create a hauntingly beautiful garden image. The choice of stitches and the assurance with which they are worked could not be bettered. Encroaching Gobelin stitch shades the sky, the water and the reflections of the topiary, whose smooth dark surface throws into contrast the dense feathery texture of the living yew foliage in the clipped outline of the birds and the vertical hedge. These are rendered in diagonal stitches in many different shades of green, which in their turn contrast with the lighter tones of the sunlit flower-strewn grass.

A limited range of tones also proves effective in the embroidery of Janet Galloway's 'Pampas Island, Friar Park, Henley on Thames', a portrait of a wonderfully idiosyncratic garden with grottoes, lakes and a Japanese garden with pools and bridges. Here the still water reflects the dark silhouettes of trees and the pampas grass along the water's edge. The upright plumes of the grass echo the trees on the skyline, and the composition shows how telling the choice of a single plant of distinctive shape can be.

The slender flowering rush and statuesque water iris make beautiful reflections, and the heart-shaped leaves of the waterlily, their ribbed undersides and long stems reaching down deep below the surface, make patterns which have inspired artists and craftsmen through the ages. In the naïve representation of *Iris pseudacorus* on page 149 the undulating water patterns interweave with the roots of the plant – an image which could be interpreted in quilting, machine embroidery or couching. A box I made inspired by these early woodcuts from the herbals was designed to represent a lily pool. The sides of the box were machine-embroidered with undulating lines of water and inter-twining roots, from which stems rose to support the leaves and flowers on the lid of the box. Here on the lid, representing the silky surface of the pool, a shimmering dragonfly skimmed the water.

Flowering rush from *Studies in Plant Form and Design* by W. Midgeley and A. E. V. Lilley (1896).

Design for a waterlily box.

'Pampas Island, Friar Park, Henley on Thames' by Janet Galloway. Free machine embroidery and appliqué on a dyed cotton evenweave ground. The water is dyed silk and chiffon applied with bondaweb, and the water plants are machine embroidered on dissolvable fabric with further hand stitches using wool, silk, cotton and linen threads, and dyed strips of silk.

11

GREENHOUSES AND CONSERVATORIES

'Who loves a garden loves a greenhouse too.
Unconscious of a less propitious clime
There blooms exotic beauty warm and snug,
While the wind whistles and the snows descend.'

William Cowper, 'The Task' (1784)

Cowper's statement is as true today as it was in 1784 when he included these lines in his long poem 'The Task'. Everyone responds to the sight and smells of a well-tended greenhouse, whether it is a modest lean-to crammed with neatly pricked out seedlings and redolent of the pungent tang of tomato foliage, or a sophisticated conservatory garlanded with plumbago and filled with the swooning scent of jasmine. In Cowper's day greenhouses were still quite rare, though the advantage of creating an artificial climate where tender plants could grow in a small enclosed world apart from the rest of the garden were well known. The greenhouses Cowper knew were the descendants of the Renaissance orangeries. These were specially built to provide winter protection for citrus trees and other decorative 'greens' like myrtles in the great terracotta pots or square wooden cases which were a decorative feature of the garden in the summer months as can be seen in the Stoke Edith hanging on page 23.

Early orangeries were built of brick with south-facing windows and tiled roofs. They were heated by stoves, 'pans of charcole', or even candles, so that the plants 'may stand warme and safe from stormes, windes, dewes, blastings, and other mischiefs'. But it was not until nearly the end of the eighteenth century that the necessity of maximum sunlight as well as warmth was understood, and overall glazing introduced to make possible the cultivation of the ever-expanding range of plants from abroad introduced by botanists like Sir Joseph Banks.

The trickle of new plants turned into a flood during the nineteenth century and plant hunters scoured the world for exotic cultivars to furnish the thousands of new greenhouses and conservatories being erected now that glass, after the repeal of the glass tax in 1845, was cheap, and developments in cast iron made lighter frameworks with narrow glazing bars possible. Greenhouses were sited in the outer garden and used to bring on annuals for 'embroidery' bedding and plants for the conservatory. The latter was designed to be an ornamental extension to the house, visible from adjacent rooms, and furnished with wicker chairs, ironwork plantholders, statues, and even fountains and pools. It was an 'absolute necessity in connection with the "House of Taste" ', as Shirley Hibberd described it in the Victorian best seller *Rustic Adornments for Homes of Taste*. And in the *Suburban Gardener* (1838), J. C. Loudon described the 'effect of a picturesque grove of climbers' seen through the glass door which led invitingly out of the everyday world of the drawing room into the more exotic atmosphere of the conservatory. As if to emphasize this, some conservatory doors were made with a central pane of plain glass surrounded by smaller stained-glass panels etched with conservatory plants like fuchsias and passion flowers – bright frames for the enticing view beyond – and an interesting idea to develop in embroidery, either in terms of the contrast between the glowing stained-glass colours – a rich deep red was much favoured – and the deep greens of the foliage beyond, or between the flat etched flowers and their exuberant living counterparts.

It was the luxurious aspect of the conservatory that made it into a cult in the nineteenth century, and it is small wonder that it was often the setting for assignations and proposals of marriage: 'The genial warmth, the fragrance of the nobler plants, and the voluptuous stillness that prevails in this enchanted spot, lull the fancy into sweet romantic dreams', wrote a visitor to the St Petersburg winter garden in 1827. This feeling of escape into an artificial paradise was even more pronounced in the great glass palaces erected in botanic gardens all over Europe and in America. 'Winter Garden' on page 154 explores the exotic plants and structure of the greenhouses in the Royal Botanic Gardens in Edinburgh. Near London you can visit the Palm House at Kew and marvel at the variety and size of the palms and climbers. You have entered a world of patterns, harmonizing and contrasting in a marvellous visual feast. There are nature's patterns in the great foliage fans of the palms and the amazing diversity of shapes and forms, not only in the leaves, but in the trunks, stems, fruit and flowers of tropical plants.

Chapter heading for the Conservatory chapter in *Rustic Adornments for Homes of Taste* by Shirley Hibberd.

Conservatory from Boitard.

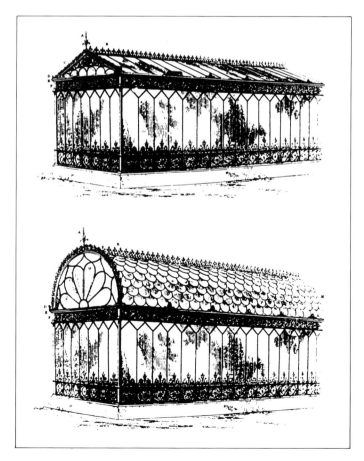

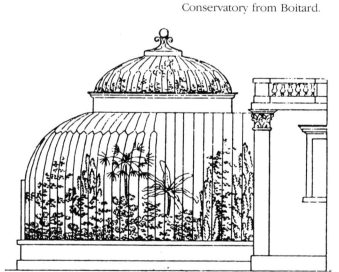

Conservatory designs with ornate ironwork from the catalogue of Walter Macfarlane & Co (1882).

'Winter Garden' by Sue Bakker, inspired by visits to the greenhouses in the Royal Botanic Gardens, Edinburgh. Machine embroidery on a sprayed and painted ground with the plants worked on vanishing muslin and applied.

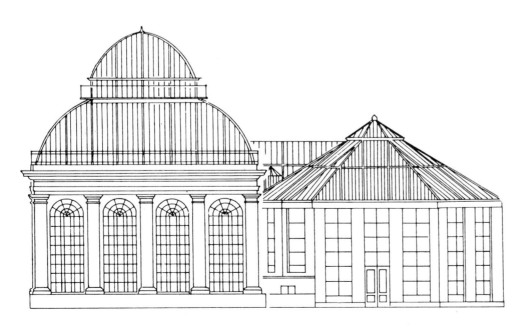

Elevation of the palm and temperate houses in the Edinburgh Royal Botanic Garden which were the inspiration for Sue Bakker's 'Winter Garden'.

'Outside from In' by Paddy Ramsay. This picture, using quilting and appliqué techniques, was made when the maker became interested in developing the ideas of the Victorian shadow box and peepshow in embroidery. Thus the garden is seen through the 'proscenium' of the elaborate arched window of the conservatory. Acetate drawn onto with overhead projection pens and Letraset, forms the ground.

Ornate conservatory with arches framing the view of palms and tropical foliage from Boitard's *l'Architecte des Jardins* (1845).

The grid formed by the greenhouse glazing bars makes an exciting contrast with the exuberant patterns of exotic foliage.

opposite Inside the conservatory in the Luxembourg Gardens. An illustration in *The Parks, Promenades and Gardens of Paris* by William Robinson.

Another feature at Kew is the huge framework of iron and glass whose verticals and horizontals create a grid and act as a foil to the free-flowing patterns of natural growth, some of which appear in formalised form in the cast ironwork. Look, for example, at the palmette or palm-leaf motif of antiquity used in the gallery railings and banisters of the spiral stairs which wind up round the central columns, white and mysterious like the uncoiling fronds of a man-made palm. Do not miss the patterns at floor level where the paving is set between cast-iron grills, some round, some rectangular.

There is inspiration for embroidery all round you, whether you look down on the plants from the galleries, or up at them and on to the roof grid, or along the paths to the glass doors and indistinct view of the gardens and water beyond. In the Princess of Wales's Greenhouse at Kew the exciting changes of level provide a succession of unusual and enthralling viewpoints, as for example when you look down on the huge leaves of the giant Amazon waterlily or see them at eye level a moment later. Paddy Ramsay's 'Outside from In' captures the mysterious allure of the winter garden, and sums up the satisfaction of outwitting the bleakest season of the year and enjoying the luxuriance of tropical plants safe from the chill of the outside garden which can be glimpsed through the glass. What better material than satin to convey the lustrous surface of the leaves, machine quilted to emphasize the central ribs and veining? Many greenhouses and conservatories fell into disrepair earlier this century when labour and heating made them too costly to heat and maintain. Now, however, they are back in fashion, smaller in scale, but still providing an extra room deliciously different from the rest of the house, where tender plants can be cultivated and enjoyed.

Patterns based on the palm-leaf motif in the Palm House at Kew.

Cross-section of a combined vine house and aviary from *The Gardener's Chronicle.*

A rectangular fern case from *Rustic Adornment.*

'The Cold Frame' by Barbara and Roy Hirst. Contemporary stumpwork by Barbara, the transfer-painted and machine-embroidered ground by Roy Hirst. The frame is ingeniously constructed with strips of silk-wrapped card, and the panes of glass are mica. The three-dimensional figure of the gardener wears needlelace clothes and this technique was also used for the seed box. The watering can and trowel are leather.

Glass in the garden tempts both gardeners and embroiderers to experiment, by trying out something new whether they choose a cloche, a frame or, more ambitiously, a special house for alpines, ferns or fruit. The framework and patterns made by the glazing bars make a good basis for a design. According to your taste you could take as your model a Victorian cast-iron structure with its wealth of ornamental detail, the striking modern shapes of a geodesic dome with panels of triangular glass, or even the dramatic 'greenhouses' in glass-walled offices where plants help bring the building alive. This is how Margaret Pascoe conceived her most original 'Towers and Flowers' panel on page 162 based on the architect's sketch for Lloyd's building in the City of London. It has often been noted that buildings like these are the direct descendants of the Elizabethan prodigy houses – of Hardwick Hall 'more glass than wall'. So it seems especially appropriate that she should choose the intricate patterns of blackwork so popular during that period, revitalising them to convey the complex outline of the new building with its central 'cage' of glass.

At the other end of the scale you might be intrigued by the miniature world of the bell jar, or the Wardian case invented by Doctor Nathaniel Bagshaw Ward, a Victorian doctor and fern enthusiast, who by chance discovered that his favourite plants flourished in the closed environment of a glass bottle where condensation was trapped on the walls

159

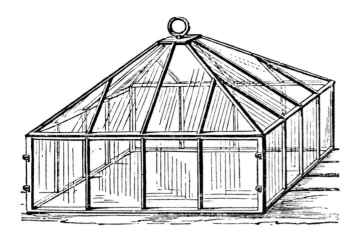

A lantern handlight used to
bring on and protect early
crops.

and ran down to water the growing medium. In the 1830s he made special glass cases with sloping sides like miniature greenhouses to send grasses and ferns on the long sea voyage to Australia. Their flourishing condition on arrival led to plants travelling all over the world in this way and speeded up the spread of new cultivars. His discovery was also taken up eagerly as a decorative feature in drawing rooms. Ornate table models were made, sometimes combining aquariums or even aviaries, and the most elaborate were set on lavishly decorated stands. It is from these cases that the terrariums of today have evolved, plainer in shape, but no less delightful in displaying a microcosm of the garden indoors.

Terrariums make ideal subjects for embroidered boxes or paperweights, indeed a three-dimensional treatment is interesting and fun to develop whether you choose a terrarium, an old-fashioned lantern handlight or a small greenhouse. You would be wise to make a model in card first, and to experiment with different arrangements of pots and plants, either set on staging or growing in the soil, to see how well they work in terms of scale. The model would serve as a pattern for the embroidery and a guide for accurate mounting. The African violets and potted plants in the terrarium and greenhouse on page 161 were machine embroidered on fabric sprayed whitish green to suggest glass. Any firm woven fabric would be suitable, and it would be interesting to try layers of semi-transparent material which would convey the effect of shading on the glass. Shadow quilting would be effective, but tricky to manipulate when making up the box. If you decided on a model with decorative ironwork, you could try machine embroidering the patterns in whip stitch or wrapping fine wire with silk and couching it down on the panels before making up.

Inside a greenhouse the trays and pots on the staging provide further subjects, varying according to the viewpoint you adopt. The patterns of pots and plants in 'The Greenhouse: Cyclamen and Tomatoes' by Eric Ravilious immediately engage the eye, and this kind of perspective view would be fascinating to treat in embroidery. Here you are looking into the greenhouse, but an equally effective view is to let the greenhouse door frame the garden, as in Stanley Spencer's 'Greenhouse and Garden' in the Ferens Art Gallery, Hull, where the open doorway frames an overgrown path leading to an orchard. In the foreground a string of large onions hangs from the roof, their rounded forms and peeling skins contrasting with the straight slats of the staging and glazing bars. But you might prefer the vertical view looking down on the pots and seed trays on the staging, possibly including the slats or gravel trays on the bench in your design. The cushions and rosettes of primulas and saxifrages in an alpine house, the filigree patterns of ferns, or the curious geometry of cacti, could be simplified to make most pleasing designs.

Illustrations of a fern and
travelling case from Nathaniel
Ward's book. *On the Imitations
of the Natural Conditions of
Plants in Closely Glazed Cases*
(1842).

'The Greenhouse: Cyclamen and Tomatoes' by Eric Ravilious. In this decorative watercolour the repetition of pots, plants and paving grills lead the eye to the distant door (© Estate of Eric Ravilious 1988, All Rights Reserved DACS).

Greenhouse and terrarium boxes designed and made by Sue Bakker and drawn by Sarah Siddall.

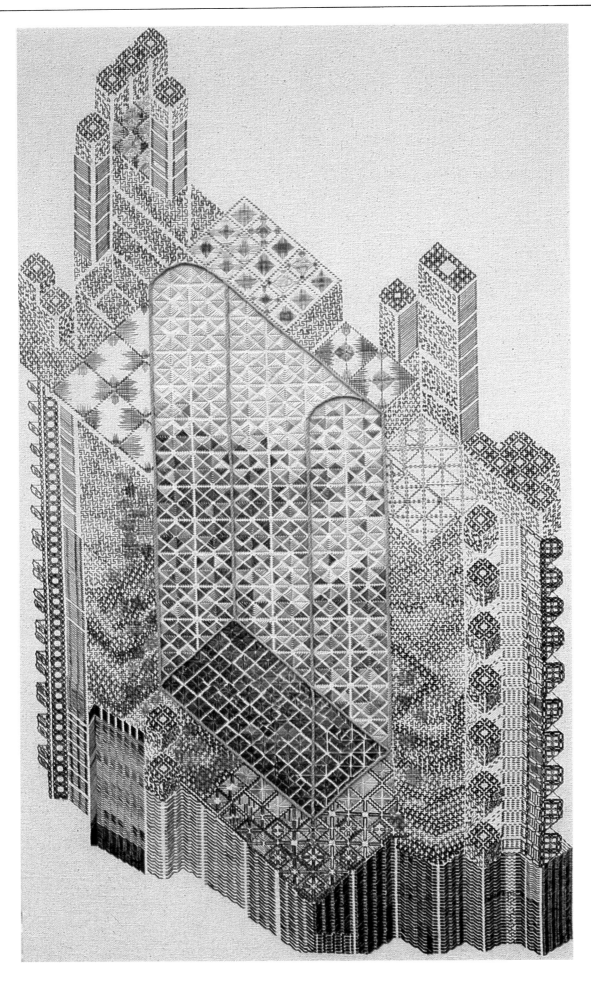

'Inside the Greenhouse' by Sara Norrish. The greenhouse structure is in seminole patchwork and the flowers combine machine and hand embroidery in a variety of threads.

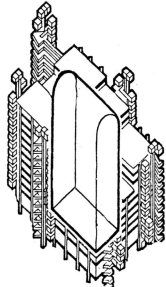

Architect's sketch which inspired the embroidery 'Flowers and Towers' by Margaret Pascoe.

opposite 'Towers and Flowers' by Margaret Pascoe. Counted thread embroidery on cream evenweave furnishing fabric. Blackwork stitches for the towers, coloured perlé threads for the flowers.

163

12

PATHS AND PAVING

*'Every garden is the better for a liberal allowance of paving.
It is required in many places, and forms the most effective
embroidery to the garden architecture, providing as it does
a groundwork which makes each feature blend with its
surroundings . . . it is a subject that allows of infinite
elaboration and the designer need have no fear of exhaust-
ing the devices to which it lends itself, alone or in
combination with other features.'*

Walter H. Godfrey, *Gardens in the Making* (1914)

Paving and other hard materials such as cobbles and gravel, which can be laid on the ground in flat patterns, are an important element in garden decoration. And, like knots, many of these patterns are interchangeable with embroidery designs, or need only the minimum of adaptation. As the designer of some of the most noted formal gardens of his day, Walter Godfrey knew exactly how to use these materials in a decorative but always practical way, and it is fascinating to find him describing their effect in terms of embroidery. He was writing at a time when labour and materials were relatively cheap, and terraces, paths and steps could be laid out in patterns of a complexity rarely possible today. Brick, stone and cobbles were often combined or laid separately in geometric patterns which adapt well in canvaswork, patchwork or quilting.

Ground plans in books like Thomas H. Mawson's *The Art and Craft of Garden Making* (1900) provide ready-made designs for square or rectangular cushions which could be worked on canvas in upright Gobelin, flat, mosaic, chequer or Scottish stitches, or on closely woven evenweave in blocks of satin stitch with the 'pointing' left unstitched. Another possibility would be to space-dye your fabric in the mellow tones of brick or tiles, or the multifarious greys and buffs of stone and then piece the patterns in patchwork. Alternatively you could tear the dyed fabric into strips of the same or differing widths and weave them into a grid. If the material was sprayed in broad stripes of the stone or brick colour alternating with narrow stripes of green, and was then torn down the centre of the green stripes, the frayed edges could suggest a network of grass or moss. Godfrey found stone 'the material most readily assimilated in the garden scheme, and trees, flowers, grass and fern all find that their colours harmonize with its pale and neutral tints'. This is equally true in embroidery, where most interesting tonal and textural experiments can be made juxtaposing the hard materials of paving and the soft material of plants so that each enhances the other. As Russell Page put it, 'the close firm texture of brick and stone warmed in the sun or glistening after a shower is a passive foil to the life and

energy of plants', an impression intensified by regular patterning in paving and freer growth in plants.

No garden designer this century understood the art of paving better than Edwin Lutyens. He was a master in devising bold patterns, many of them based on circles or squares, in well chosen materials. Russell Page describes a garden at Mothecombe House in Devon 'where he made panels banded with stone and filled with slates set on edge in cement to make a striated surface which looked like fine dark grey tweed'. In embroidery it would be interesting to develop this woven image either in needleweaving or pattern darning; or you might convey the striated effect by folding and pleating two or three layers of semi-transparent material and using them as units in a patchwork design. Random paving stones in a terrace, path or courtyard also work well in patchwork, with tiny plants set in crevices worked in free stitchery to provide small areas of detail.

In the real garden, a terrace has the function of marking the transition between the hard lines of the house and the soft volumes and spaces of the garden. From the terrace, paths, steps and walks provide access to the various parts of the garden, drawing you and your eyes onwards, leading you from one feature to another. You can tell something about the character of a garden you intend to visit simply by looking at the paths on the ground plan. In a well planned garden they act as lines of communication and unify the design. Compare for instance the formality of the layout in Thomas Hill's *The Gardener's Labyrinth* (1577), where a broad walk runs round the garden and clear, straight paths divide the beds, with the informal, indeed mysterious labyrinth conjured up by the winding paths in Batty Langley's *New Principles of Gardening* (1728). The latter book described the transition from the 'stiff regular garden' to one which presented new and natural scenes to our view at every step'. His paths meandered between groves of evergreens, fruit trees and shrubs, along 'purling streams' and into pleasant glades where you might find the entrance to a grotto or a charming ornamental building which you would 'surprisingly come to' at the turn of the path.

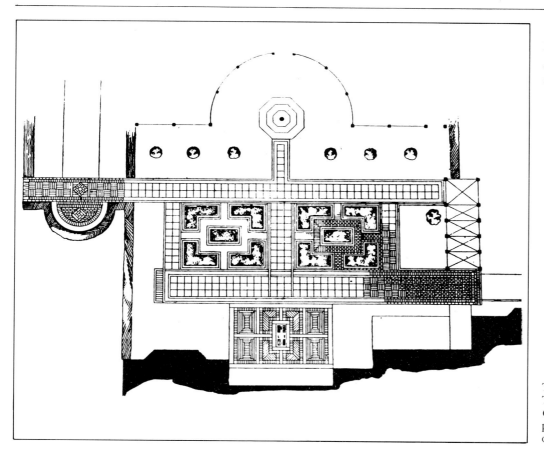

In Mawson's plan for the paved court of the Grange, Wraysbury, bricks and wood blocks are combined in patterns resembling canvaswork.

These paving patterns from Thomas Mawson's *The Art and Craft of Garden Making* suggest patchwork, quilting, appliqué or canvaswork.

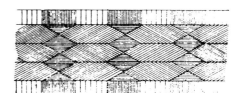

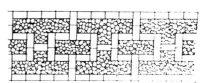

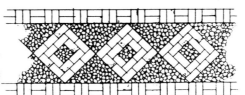

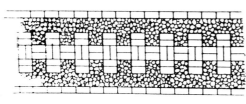

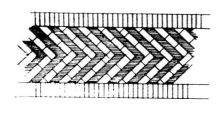

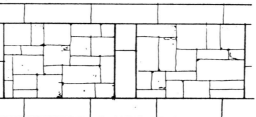

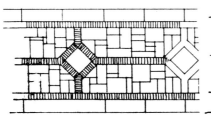

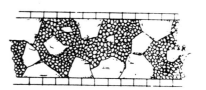

'Crazy Paved Path' by Pam Watts. Canvaswork panel inspired by low-growing plants in the maker's garden in Surrey. The paving stones are painted suede applied with straight stitches, with French knots to suggest encroaching plants creeping between them. Chenille and a variety of other threads in different textures and tones of green, some worked in Ghiordes knot, create hummocks and cushion-like plants. Picots and detached buttonhole bars render individual leaves.

opposite 'Cottage Garden' by Jennifer Wilson. Machine quilting and appliqué on painted calico with added surface stitchery.

Illustration from the title page of *Down the Garden Path* by Beverley Nichols (1932).

The maner of watering with a Pumpe in a Tubbe.

In this woodcut from *The Gardener's Labyrinth*, the straight paths divide the beds neatly for easy weeding. Note the combination of plan and perspective, and the giant bees emerging from the skeps in the top-right corner.

This type of walk was probably made of beaten earth or grass and was essentially informal, like the one described by the Reverend William Mason in a poem about his garden at Nuneham Courtenay in 1770:

Smooth simple path! Whose undulating line
With sidelong tufts of flowery fragrance crown'd
Plain in its neatness spans my garden round.

It is easy to imagine how pleasant it was to walk along such an enticing path, stopping from time to time to admire and enjoy the flowers. In embroidery the winding paths on ground plans make interesting linear patterns which could be worked in corded quilting, couching or outline stitches.

The materials and detailed design of the path can give a sense of direction, and determine your pace along it. Bricks set longwise in a stretcher-bond pattern will make you hurry, whereas a more static pattern set out in broad, squarish flagstones will make you linger, especially if the path runs between well-planted borders. If you decide to treat paths and paving pictorially rather than as flat pattern, do take this into account and make it work to your advantage. Experiment, altering the direction of your stitches, and the spacing and grouping of blocks of stitches. If you decide on a perspective view, make the patterning a feature of the design.

The embroidered path can suggest the mood of the garden or reflect your mood as you walk along it. Consider stepping stones for instance – a marvellous subject for embroidery, both as flat pattern and in pictorial representation. In the real garden they are often taken for granted as a short cut across the lawn, but they cry out for more

opposite In complete contrast the paths in this plan from Batty Langley's *New Principles of Gardening* wriggle and meander, enticing the visitor to follow them and promising pretty surprises along the way. Quilting would be an obvious choice here.

The inset brick patterns add interest to this path from the *Art and Craft of Garden Making.*

opposite 'Summer Sunday' by Juliet Wheeler. Collage picture with some surface stitchery, depicting the maker and her husband in their Sussex garden. The paving stones are cut from a variety of materials overlaid with net. The urns are planted with nasturtiums.

170

These Chinese paving patterns immediately suggest trapunto and corded quilting.

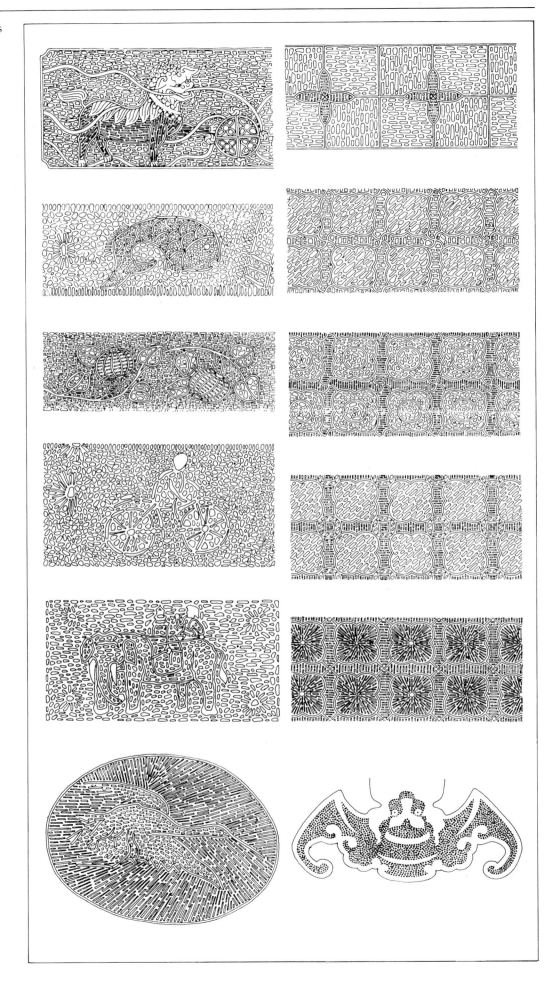

sophisticated treatment. Their potential was properly understood in Japan where, from the ninth century, to quote Christopher Thacker in *The History of Gardens*:

> Stepping stones, unconsidered trifles in many western gardens, mere means of avoiding the mud, assume extraordinary significance in the Japanese tea garden. Not only do they indicate our path, but their spacing and grouping dictate our pace and attitude. If the stones are small and placed close together, we may for example, walk carefully, giving our attention to the stones themselves; if we reach a larger broad stone, we may stop to look up and admire the new prospect which is before us.

Stepping stones vary in size and shape and can be made from stone, or wood cut from a tree-trunk. They can be set in sand, pebbles, grass or moss, and they can lead the way over shallow water. In embroidery, concentrate on the subtle harmonies and contrasts of texture and tone between, for example grey-green lichen-encrusted stones framed by springy, bright-green moss. In Jennifer Wilson's path embroidery on page 166 the large paving slabs are a feature of the design and are varied in tone by spraying the material. Further surface interest is given by quilting round their shapes, and contrasting their smoothness with the varied textures of machine-embroidered plants.

The curved shapes and smooth rounded surfaces of stones, cobbles and pebbles lend themselves well to quilting. The elaborate mosaic paving designs for paths and courtyards in Chinese gardens provide interesting patterns, some geometric, some free flowing. The fish, flowers, butterflies and bats (the symbol of good luck) made from pebbles, tiles and broken stones form a highly decorative surface. Corded quilting for outlining and trapunto quilting for raising the pebble could be striking, but wadded quilting would be more practical and comfortable for cushions or bedspreads. Transfer paints used on thin paper placed over the design would enable you to transfer a complex pattern to your ground for quilting by hand or machine. A pleasing effect could be created if the pattern was quilted in monochrome and then lightly sprayed in a slightly deeper tone to highlight the raised surface of the cobbles.

Simple pebble mosaics have been used for paths in English gardens since the seventeenth century, often designed with decorative borders and motifs. Elongated pebbles set diagonally look remarkably like raised chain band, and if this stitch were chosen the path area could be filled in with detached chain stitches following the fan or swirling patterns of the cobbles.

Blackwork effectively renders the pattern of paving stones in this view of Kew Palace by Mary Grierson.

173

13

GARDEN ORNAMENT

Ornament, in the shape of statues, vases, seats, trellis and wirework, can add enormously to the beauty and atmosphere of a garden, provided its position is chosen with care, and its scale is appropriate to its surroundings. In the real garden it can be used to bring out the character and reinforce the plan; embroiderers who study how this is done will find the knowledge invaluable when it comes to working out their own designs. Statues and vases, for example, can be placed to emphasize the order and symmetry of the formal garden. Set out along walks, terraces and steps, beside a pool, or in pairs by a gateway, they direct your steps and focus your attention, either on the statues or vases themselves, or on a particular feature or view. A single urn on a pedestal or a statue in an informal setting can act as a focal point, drawing your steps and thoughts towards it.

The solid forms and modelled surfaces of statues and vases stand out in terms of mass, colour and texture against the looser shapes of the grass, plants and hedges of their setting. This contrast – the solidity of stone, earthenware or lead against the fragility of vegetation; of mass, the sheer weight of the ornaments against the thinness and delicacy of petals, and leaves and blades of grass – is often highly marked. In embroidery the exploration of this contrast is fascinating. The techniques of quilting and the raised methods of stumpwork produce rounded forms which can be balanced and enhanced by surface stitchery, as can be seen in Jennifer Wilson's 'Émile' opposite and Margaret Hall's 'Girl in a Garden' below, in which the padded form of the ornate vase stands out from the bright miscellany of flowers worked in detached buttonhole stitch.

'Girl in a Garden' by Margaret Hall. Machine and hand embroidery on Thai silk. Stitches include detached buttonhole, whipped running, seeding and couching, all in silk thread.

'Emile' by Jennifer Wilson. Machine and hand embroidery combined on a painted and sprayed ground. The statue stands guard at the entrance to the garden grotto.

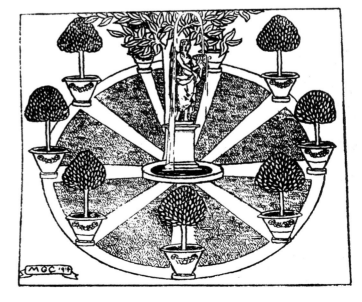

A symmetrical arrangement of pots round a fountain from *Gardens: Their Form and Design*.

175

Well-balanced pots and vases of flowers including a lead cistern. The patterns on these beautiful containers make interesting subjects for corded quilting.

Vases and pots are one of the most versatile forms of garden ornament, as pleasing and adaptable in embroidery as in the real garden. In texture, shape and colour they are astonishingly diverse. Marble and terracotta are not simply white or red, but endlessly varied by age, by the weather or the growth of lichen and moss. Lead can feature at any point in the spectrum from silver to darkest grey. Urns, troughs and pots, and statues too, whether marble, terracotta or lead, can be black when seen in silhouette or, when the light is right, part black in the shade and part colour, rich with the solidity of the object. You can treat vases and pots singly or in groups. For town dwellers, pots on a balcony or roof – even an old stone trough or a tall pot with holes for a dozen herbs – can become a garden in miniature, and an inspiration for embroidery of a most rewarding kind.

'The love of plants in pots seems alive in all true gardeners. Is it the sense of protection of something small, more helpless than ourselves, that we and children feel in tending them?' asked Frances Wolseley in *Gardens Their Form and Design*. Certainly it is a centuries-old tradition, and beautiful examples can be seen in Egyptian and classical art. Herself an admirer of formal gardens, especially those of Italy, Lady Wolseley liked to see pots of graduated height placed in symmetrical patterns which were especially beautiful viewed from above, with roses and lilies forming 'circles and ovals of colour'. We have already discussed how

Troughs and pots seen from above, the rim patterns making simple frames for the flowers.

well this viewpoint works in embroidery, and the juxtaposed rims of pots – some plain, some patterned – could make the basis of a most effective design. The rims could be made from cut-out squares, circles, rectangles or ovals of felt or Vilene covered with fabric, applied to a firm background. Quilting the shape would be another possibility. An old stone trough, its broad rim mottled with lichen and algae, would be a particularly interesting subject. Seen from above the rim would provide a frame for the plants and make pleasing contrasts of texture with them.

In the real garden, troughs are delightful because they bring choice alpines and other tiny plants nearer to eye level, where their form and character can be studied and enjoyed. In *The Contemplative Gardener* (1940), Jason Hill describes the pleasure of growing plants in containers like this as 'doll's house gardening', 'a kind of embroidery', using jewel-bright flowers. He suggested miniature saxifrage, tiny cranesbills and campanulas with a background of creeping thyme. The small scale and precious contents of such trough gardens suggest intricate embroidery and the use of fine materials and complex stitches. The raised methods of stumpwork would be fun to try out, especially if the trough contained cushion- or dome-shaped succulents like houseleeks which could be worked in detached buttonhole stitch lightly padded with wool.

It is essential in both the real garden and in embroidery that plant and container complement each other in scale, texture and shape, and that they suit and enhance their surroundings. Notice how the mop-headed orange trees in their elaborate containers match up in pairs outside the Stoke Edith Orangery on page 23 and note how this arrangement emphasizes the symmetry of the layout and adds to the decorative appeal of the hanging. Not nearly enough thought is given to this art, and many gardens are let down by dull, ill-assorted marriages of quite unsuited

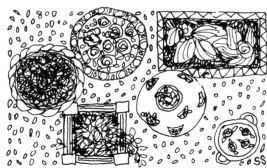

plants and pots. You will find inspiration in gardens like Tintinhull in Somerset and Sissinghurst in Kent, where plants and pots seem always to be perfectly matched and imaginatively placed. At Sissinghurst, for example, containers in terracotta, copper, stone, glazed earthenware, lead and marble are filled with an unusually wide range of flowers, including clematis cunningly trained in garlands round a tall vase, and simple white-flowered daisy trees in elaborate terracotta pots flanking a seat. Everywhere the pots are placed against a background which enhances them, whether it is yew, brick or stone; or they are framed in arches and openings making perfect garden pictures. I would myself like to plan and execute a series of small embroideries based on the pots at Sissinghurst, or even, on a larger scale, make a screen with a row of alternating pots and trees as in the Lime Walk.

There is much to be said for working in series, and trying out variations on garden themes. In my garden I have some Victorian wirework plant stands for holding rows of pots, and these I have embroidered many times, changing the background, the pots and the flowers with each new piece. These plant stands, and the equally pretty Victorian seats of similar construction, were made by bending wire into delicate tracery patterns which transpose well in outline stitches, couching or machine whip stitch. Shadow quilting might also be tried, cutting out simple pot and plant shapes in fabric and snippets of thread and placing them between an upper layer of organdie or semi-transparent silk on a firmer backing of calico or cotton. Wrought- or cast-iron seats could be worked in outline too; or you could try wrapping fine wire with silk thread or stranded cotton and couching it down as suggested in Chapter 4.

Carnations supported by bent osiers in a lightly decorated pot from Bock's herbal of 1546. This practical and ornamental arrangement can be seen in the Tudor Garden at Southampton and would be interesting to try out in free stitchery with silk-wrapped wire hoops and much-simplified foliage.

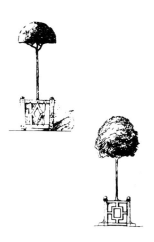

Box trees in wooden cases from *The Art and Craft of Gardening.*

'Jardinière by a Window' by the author. Real and imaginary elements are combined in this picture. The Victorian plant holder is worked in machine whip stitch as is the trug. The secateurs and flowers are stitched by hand in coloured silks, and there is further light hand stitchery on the painted view based on a picture by the Polish painter, Balthus, whose landscapes have a compellingly mysterious quality.

opposite 'The Croquet Lawn at Castle Drogo' by Janet Haigh. The silk ground is painted and stitched freely in unplied Japanese yarn. The maker was influenced by the effects of light on foliage in Seurat's paintings, and to render the rhythms of light and shade on yew and grass the strands of silk were pulled apart and reblended with four different tones in each needleful.

Diverse shaped vases and topiary trees in a colonnade of trellis work from the *Hypnerotomachia*. These simple outlines suggest appliqué or outline stitches with the panels in laid work.

In a garden a seat acts as an invitation to rest, beckoning you towards it. Most seats, whether made of wood, stone or metal, look well against the dark-green background of a hedge, as you can see in Janet Haigh's picture 'The Croquet Lawn at Castle Drogo'. The design of the seat, by Edwin Lutyens, is famous; and here its elegant outline is rendered in neat satin stitches which stand out firmly against the looser stitchery of the hedge. Whatever background you choose, whether a hedge, a wall, or a romantic profusion of

A design for a threefold screen based on the Lime Walk at Sissinghurst, where in spring bulbs fill the pots and spaces in the paving.

midsummer roses, make sure it plays its part in the overall composition in terms of colour, texture and shape. At the end of my garden I have a Gothic seat which stands against a background of ivy growing up the wall. The seat badly needs repainting, but for several seasons I have not known what colour to use. A pure white seems too glaring, and so I debate whether to have a beigy stone colour or a bluish grey. Before deciding, I shall first make an experiment in embroidery. I shall make a picture of the scene using machine whip stitch on watercolour painted silk, balancing the tones to make sure the tracery pattern of the seat stands out sufficiently against the ivy. In Claude Monet's garden at Giverny, a vivid emerald green is used on the metalwork arches and plant supports which add vertical interest all over the garden. This shade of green has no counterpart in nature; but it balances perfectly the intensity of flower colour, and its contrast with the varied greens of trees and foliage makes a striking visual effect.

The patterns of wrought- and cast-iron seats and Victorian wirework plantholders transpose well in outline stitches or machine whip stitch.

'The Secret Garden at
Tyninghame' by Anne
Kinniment. Machine
embroidered picture of the
elegant treillage arbour in this
East Lothian garden. The
ground is dyed and painted,
and hand embroidery is added
to the machine work.

'Green Trellis' by Vicky Lugg. Canvaswork panel with ribbon outlining the pattern of the trellis and the plants worked in French knots and straight stitches in threads of varied textures. Border in mosaic stitch.

This garden house of treillage from W. Godfrey's *Gardens in the Making* could frame a simple view.

Trellis can create illusionary perspectives as in this example from *Gardens: Their Form and Design.*

Trellis frames the view of the flower garden at Valleyfield, Fife, designed by Humphry Repton.

Trellis arches are another versatile form of garden ornament, well suited to picture- or pattern-making in embroidery. The regular square and diamond patterns of traditional wooden trellis form ready-made grids which act as a foil to the informal growth of plants. The angular quality of the patterns makes them particularly useful for canvas-work, as can be seen in the many small-scale garden views in Elizabethan valances, where enclosures, alleys and arbours, some interwoven with roses and honeysuckle, lend an air of mystery and romance to the scene.

Trellis makes possible all sorts of interesting visual surprises both in large and small gardens. For this reason it has been used since Roman times either to partly conceal some garden view, or to create illusionary effects of distance and depth. In a large garden it can, as a framework, divide the foreground from the open space beyond; in a small one it can make the closely spaced areas more separate and more inviting. Many of these effects can be developed in embroidery. You could base your design on the intricate patterns of seventeenth-century trellis known as 'treillage' (the word describes the more elaborate architectural use of trellis), concentrating on the linear quality and using an evenweave ground. This would be fascinating to try out in blackwork. Again, you could start from a single panel of trellis and bring out the contrast of texture and shape between the trellis and the plants, as in Vicky Lugg's 'Green

Trellis' on page 183 where the strong framework is outlined in narrow green ribbon whose shiny surface stands out from the matt threads of the irregularly shaped plants. Trellis comes in shades of dark brown, or it can be painted white or stained green, and the colour you choose plays an important part in the composition.

In the real garden, trellis can transform a flat wall or courtyard by cunning use of perspective; in embroidery you could simulate these effects using narrow ribbon, cord or braid. In a garden, look through a trellis screen near to and from a distance; the effects are quite different, but equally tempting for embroidery. Near to, the square- or diamond-shaped holes made by the slats of the trellis form a series of frames permitting selected views of the space beyond; further away the space is veiled by the lattice and becomes indistinct, and your attention is drawn to the trellis itself and the plants it supports. Lines in Thomas Mawson's *The Art and Craft of Garden Making* (1900) perceptively sum up the uses and charm of trellis, and of the other forms of ornament described in this chapter:

In the laying out of a garden . . . there is a certain seductive mystery gained by partly concealing and judiciously screening some parts from immediate view. By this means the imagination is tempted to conjecture the presence of hidden delights beyond, and this interest is quickened in expectation of some further enchantment.

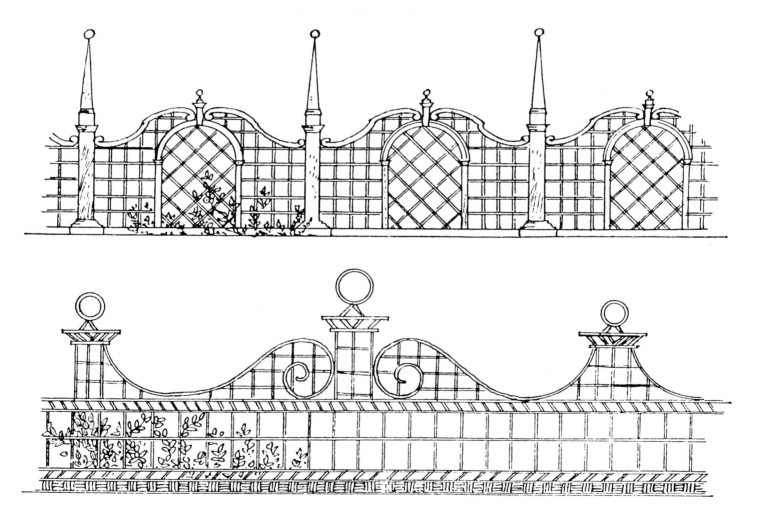

Seventeenth-century designs for trellis fences from *Garden Craft in Europe* by H. Inigo Triggs (1913).

185

POSTSCRIPT

Gardens and embroidery are essentially personal creations. As Lady Wolseley so aptly put it: 'A garden is amongst many delights the clear mirror of soul and character, for each owner is here reflected in his true colours. In the house he may dissemble, take us in, but in the garden all is honesty, because no deceit gains admission.'

I hope the images and quotations in this book have provided inspiration for your embroidery, and made your garden and those you visit of even greater interest than before. My own garden and my embroidery have been somewhat neglected this year while I have been writing and searching for illustrations. On 16 October hurricane-force winds brought down millions of trees in south-east England, amongst them the golden acacia illustrated on page 59, then at the height of its autumn display. I shall plant another, but I doubt if it will reach the size and splendour of the original in my lifetime. The making of my embroidered version gave me particular satisfaction; it was a sketch, done in haste before the leaves should lose their brilliance or the flowers in the vase fade away. Now it is a poignant reminder of the fragility of gardens, a ghost of lost radiance, and an affirmation of the pleasures embroidery affords both mind and eye.

31 October 1987

'My Gardening Year' by Maureen Pratt. The year begins with the maker reading a seed catalogue, she then plants seeds, watches them sprout, weeds and tends the plants. In late autumn the display is over and she sinks exhausted but happy in her chair with another year in the garden completed. The black dog is her constant companion and takes part at every stage. The illustration above is from *Down the Garden Path* by Beverley Nichols (1932).

BIBLIOGRAPHY

Many of the out of print books mentioned in the text can be consulted in the Library of the Victoria and Albert Museum, London, which is open to the public, or in the Lindley Library of the Royal Horticultural Society (members only). This list includes only books which are currently available.

Garden books

For pleasure and inspiration

Angel, Heather. *A View from a Window* (Unwin Hyman, 1988)

Balston, Michael. *The Well Furnished Garden*. Perceptive chapters on design and ornament followed by an invaluable catalogue of garden features illustrated in drawings and photographs (Mitchell Beazley, 1986)

Grierson, Mary. *An English Florilegium*. Watercolours of the plants connected with the Tradescant family of gardeners in the seventeenth century (Thames & Hudson, 1987)

Hill, Thomas. *The Gardener's Labyrinth* of 1577 edited by Richard Mabey. The first popular garden book now happily in print again (Oxford University Press, 1987)

Joyes, Claire. *Claude Monet, His Life at Giverny* (Thames & Hudson, 1986)

Lloyd, Christopher. *The Year at Great Dixter*. A personal, evocative account of the garden and through it the gardener (Viking, 1987)

Midda, Sara. *In and Out of the Garden*. Study of old garden books inspired many of the illustrations in this enchanting book (Sidgwick & Jackson, 1981)

Page, Russell. *The Education of a Gardener*. Original and thought provoking, but also full of practical advice on design (1962, reprinted Penguin, 1985)

Scott James, Anne. *Sissinghurst, the Making of a Garden* (Michael Joseph, 1974, reprinted 1987)

Thacker, Christopher. *The History of Gardens*. A profusely illustrated classic work bringing alive the gardens and gardeners of the past (Croome Helm, 1979, reprinted 1985)

Vita Sackville-West's Gardening Book. A collection of articles selected by Philippa Nicholson (Michael Joseph, 1987)

Books by and about Gertrude Jekyll

Wood and Garden (1899, reprinted 1987) and *Home and Garden* (1900, reprinted 1986) are good introductions to her writing; both have been reprinted by the Antique Collectors Club.

A Gardener's Testament (ed Francis Jekyll and G. C. Taylor) is a selection of articles and notes illustrated by photographs taken at Munstead Wood (Papermac, 1984)

Gertrude Jekyll on Gardening, an anthology edited with a commentary by Penelope Hobhouse. Explains her planting schemes for gardeners today (Papermac, 1983)

Brown, Jane. *Gardens of a Golden Afternoon*. Describes the partnership between Miss Jekyll and Edwin Lutyens (Viking, 1982)

Edwards, Joan. *Gertrude Jekyll Embroiderer, Gardener and Craftsman*. A short biography which tells of Miss Jekyll's interest in embroidery (Bayford Books, 1981)

Design and features

Brookes, John. *The Garden Book*. Well illustrated with easy to follow advice on plan making and instructive perspectives and plans of the same garden (Dorling Kindersley, 1984)

Hicks, David. *Garden Design*. Practical suggestions for formal garden design with excellent black and white photographs, some with design ideas and improvements overlaid on tracing paper (Routledge & Kegan Paul, 1982)

Rose, Graham. *The Small Garden Planner*. Plans in line and watercolour suggestive of stitches and designs (Mitchell Beazley, 1987)

Strong, Roy. *Creating Small Gardens*. Well drawn plans which would make good patterns (Octopus, 1986)

Thomas, Graham Stuart (ed.) *Recreating the Period Garden*. Chapters on plan making, topiary, ornament, paths and water gardens (Collins, 1984)

Verey, Rosemary. *Classic Garden Design*. How to adapt and recreate the gardens of the past with chapters on topiary, knots, paths and herb gardens (Viking, 1984)

Herbals

Arber, Agnes. *Herbals, their Origin and Evolution* (Cambridge Science Classics, 1986)

Blunt, Wilfrid and Raphael, Sandra. *The Illustrated Herbal*. Many little known illustrations from manuscripts and herbals (Weidenfeld & Nicholson, 1979)

de Pass, Crispin. *Hortus Floridus*, 1615 (Minerva Press, 1974)

Hatton, Ralph. *The Handbook of Plant and Floral Ornament*. (First published 1909 as *The Craftsman's Plant Book*.) Indispensable source of plant designs from the herbals with an interesting introductory chapter on their use as elements of design (Dover, 1960)

Herb gardens

Cooper, Guy, Taylor, Gordon and Boursnell, Clive. *English Herb Gardens*. Beautiful photographs of herb gardens, many taken from interesting viewpoints, with useful glossary of herbs (Weidenfeld & Nicholson, 1986)

Garland, Sarah. *The Herb Garden* (Windward, 1984)

Greenhouses

Boniface, Priscilla. *The Winter Garden.* Evocative photographs of Victorian and Edwardian conservatories and greenhouses (HMSO, 1982)

Koppelkam, Stefan. *Glasshouses and Wintergardens of the Nineteenth Century.* Superb photographs of ironwork and plants (Granada, 1981)

Colour

Hobhouse, Penelope. *Colour in Your Garden.* Informative chapter on colour theory and inspiring photographs showing how to use colour to create perspective effects (Collins, 1985)

Jekyll, Gertrude. *Colour Schemes for the Flower Garden,* 1909 (The Antique Collectors' Club, 1982)

Topiary

Lacey, Geraldine. *Creating Topiary* (Garden Art Press, 1987)

Islamic Gardens

Brookes, John. *Gardens of Paradise, the History and Design of the Great Islamic Gardens.* Photographs of existing gardens and Mughal and Persian miniatures showing complex layouts of water channels, chadars and tanks (Weidenfeld & Nicholson, 1987)

Embroidery books

It is not within the scope of this book to describe in practical detail the many different techniques suggested in the text; numerous excellent books on the subject are available. However, books I have found particularly useful are listed below.

General

Coleman, Anne. *Creative Embroidery for Beginners.* Well planned with a useful section on transfer paints and dyes (Bishopsgate Press, 1986)

Embroiderers' Guild Practical Study Group. *Needlework School.* A first-rate introduction for beginners, equally worthwhile for the more experienced; beautifully designed with practical hints on mounting and framing and with sections on appliqué, patchwork, stumpwork, quilting, stitching on evenweave and machine embroidery (Windward, 1984)

Warren, Verina. *Landscape in Embroidery.* Covers a variety of methods all described with exemplary clarity. The chapters on colour, applying colour to fabric by painting or spraying, machine embroidery techniques and mounting and presentation are encouraging for beginners in their step by step approach and nonetheless stimulating for the more experienced (Batsford, 1986)

Stitches

Beaney, Jan. *Stitches, New Approaches* (Batsford, 1987)

Campbell Harding, Val. *Textures in Embroidery* (Batsford, 1985)

Christie, Grace. *Samplers and Stitches.* A pleasure to read as well as to use (1920, reprinted Batsford, 1986)

Snook, Barbara. *Embroidery Stitches* (Dryad, 1985)

Thomas, Mary. *A Dictionary of Embroidery Stitches* (Hodder & Stoughton, 1985)

Blackwork

Geddes, Elizabeth and McNeill, Moyra. *Blackwork Embroidery* (Dover, 1976)

Pascoe, Margaret. *Blackwork Embroidery, Design and Technique* (Batsford, 1986)

Canvaswork

Gray, Jennifer. *Canvaswork* (Batsford, 1985)

Rhodes, Mary. *Dictionary of Canvas Work Stitches* (Batsford, 1985)

Machine Embroidery

Clucas, Joy. *The New Machine Embroidery* (David & Charles, 1987)

McNeill, Moyra. *Machine Embroidery Lace and See-through Techniques.* Clear instructions on using vanishing muslin, pulled thread by machine, and embroidery on dissolvable fabrics (Batsford, 1985)

Patchwork

Pyman, Kit. *Every kind of Patchwork* (Search Press, 1983)

Quilting

Short, Eirian. *Quilting, Technique, Design and Application* (Batsford, 1979)

Drawing

Camp, Jeffery. *Draw, How to Master the Art.* Marvellous book with foreword by David Hockney extolling practice of copying as a 'first-rate way to learn to look because it is looking through somebody else's eyes, at the way that person saw something and ordered it around on paper'. Teaches us to see the world around us through the marks of past artists, encouraging the most faint hearted to discover the pleasure of drawing. The sections on tone and recession, perspective, apertures, trees and gardens are inspiring for garden embroidery (Dorling Kindersley, 1981)

Periodical

Embroidery, the quarterly magazine of the Embroiderers' Guild contains information on classes and suppliers of some of the less readily available materials mentioned in this book such as special fabric paints and dissolvable materials. Write to Embroidery Magazine, PO Box 42B, East Molesey, Surrey KT8 9BB.

Classes

Classes are run by the Embroiderers' Guild at Hampton Court and the Royal School of Needlework in London, and by local education authorities all over the country.

GARDENS
OF SPECIAL INTEREST
TO EMBROIDERERS

This list is limited to gardens open to the public. It is essential to check opening times in *The Guide to Historic Houses, Castles and Gardens Open to the Public*, available from British Leisure Publications, Windsor Court, East Grinstead House, East Grinstead, West Sussex RH19 1XA before making a visit.

Gardens whose design, planting and features are of exceptional interest to embroiderers
Athelhampton Manor, Dorset
Barnsley House, Glos
Blickling Hall, Norfolk
Cranborne Manor, Dorset
Goodnestone, Kent
Great Dixter, East Sussex
Hampton Court, Greater London
Hatfield House, Herts
Heale House, Wilts
Hidcote Manor, Glos
Port Lympne, Kent
Sissinghurst Castle, Kent
Tintinhull House, Somerset
White Barn House (the Beth Chatto Garden), Essex

Knot gardens
Hall Place, Stratford-on-Avon, Warwickshire
Little Moreton Hall, Cheshire
Moseley Old Hall, West Midlands
Tradescant Garden, Lambeth, London
Tudor Garden, Southampton, Hants

Also at Barnsley House, Cranborne Manor, Hampton Court, Hatfield House

Parterres
Ashdown House, Oxon
Chatsworth, Derbyshire
Cliveden, Berks
Drummond Castle, Perthshire
Ham House, Greater London
Oxburgh Hall, Norfolk
Pitmedden, Aberdeenshire

Mazes
Glendurgan House, Cornwall
Greys Court, Oxon
Leeds Castle, Kent
Longleat House, Wilts
Tatton Park, Cheshire

Also at Hampton Court, Hatfield House

Topiary
Hall Place, Bexley, Greater London
Hever Castle, Kent
Knightshayes Court, Devon
Levens Hall, Cumbria
Nymans Garden, East Sussex
Packwood House, Warwickshire

Also at Great Dixter, Hidcote Manor

Herb gardens
Chenies Manor, Bucks
Emmanuel College, Cambridge
Fulham Palace, London
Hardwick Hall, Derbyshire
Knebworth House, Herts
Moseley Old Hall, West Midlands
Scotney Castle, Kent

Also at Cranborne Manor, Sissinghurst Castle

Vegetables and fruit
Erddig, Clwyd
Westbury Court Garden, Glos
West Green House, Hartley Witney, Hants

Also at Barnsley House

Greenhouses
Bicton Gardens, Devon
Chatsworth, Derbyshire
Glasgow Botanic Garden
Kew Gardens, Greater London
Royal Botanic Gardens, Edinburgh
Sefton Park, Liverpool
Syon House, Greater London

INDEX

ACKNOWLEDGEMENTS

This book could not have been written without the cooperation of all the embroiderers who allowed me to reproduce their work, and I would like to thank them most sincerely for their unfailing generosity and help. I would also like to thank Sarah Siddall for carefully interpreting my ideas in her many line drawings and adding her own witty touches. I am also most grateful to photographer Dudley Moss and to Dr Brent Elliott at the Lindley Library, Royal Horticultural Society. At David & Charles I am indebted to Pam Griffiths and Brenda Morrison for much help and encouragement.

Picture Credits

Academy Editions, page 172; Mr & Mrs Bazeley, 127 above; Bodleian Library, 16; T. Bowes, 115 below; William Briggs, 98 above; British Library 132 centre; British Museum, 47 below; John Brookes, 41 above; Nic Broomhead, 87 above, 143; Wendy Brose collection, 71; Country Life, 84 above; Bill Dodd, 63, 123; John Galloway, 18, 111 above, 151; Sally Harris, 151; Lindley Library, 57, 81, 105 above & below, 125 below left, 128 above, 129, 136, 153 above, 160 centre & below, 169; Christopher Lloyd, 7 below; Danny McClure, 55 above, 146 above, 154 above; Methuen & Co, 20 above; Mr & Mrs G. Mole, 38; Dudley Moss, 10, 19, 27 above, 30 above, 31 below, 43, 50 above & below, 51, 66, 67, 75, 91, 95 above, 95 below right, 107, 134, 147, 159, 171; Oxford University Press, 41 below; J.E. Pascoe, 162; Keith Pattison, 63, 123, 155 above; Elizabeth Scarf, 155 above; Richard Sorrell, 7 above; Sotheby's, 8, 42 above; Jessica Strang, 11; Tate Gallery, 161 above; Lady Emma Tennant, 58; Christopher Thacker, 35, 58, 59, 70, 74 above, 79 above, 99 below, 138 above, 167 above; Transglobe, 125 above; Victoria and Albert Museum, 11 above, 30, 147; the Warden and Fellows of All Souls College, Oxford, 69 below.

Printed Sources

Jason Hill, *The Contemplative Gardener*, Mrs Jillian Leech. Russell Page, *The Education of a Gardener*, William Collins. *Vita Sackville-West's Gardening Book*, Michael Joseph.

British Library Cataloguing in Publication Data

Beck, Thomasina
 The embroiderer's garden
 1. Embroidery. Special subjects. Gardens.
 Designs
 I. Title
 746.44

 ISBN 0-7153-9117-8

© Thomasina Beck 1988

First published 1988
Second impression 1988
Third impression 1989
Fourth impression 1990

Typeset by Typesetters (Birmingham) Ltd
and printed in West Germany
by Mohndruck GmbH
for David & Charles plc
Brunel House Newton Abbot Devon

Distributed in the United States by
Sterling Publishing Co. Inc.
387 Park Avenue South, New York, NY 10016-8810